AI Agents

Through the company of Zero

Daniel Locke

ISBN: 9798310773981

Table of Contents

Prologue

I've always been fascinated by technology—how it evolves, how it reshapes industries, and how it changes what's possible. My journey into AI and automation wasn't a straight path. It wasn't something I planned. But looking back, every step I took led me here.

I started my career in the traditional business world, where success meant long hours, large teams, and complex operations. The idea of running a company without employees or managers seemed like science fiction. But over the years, I watched technology transform businesses, making them more efficient, more automated, and less dependent on human labor. What once seemed impossible started to feel inevitable.

Then AI changed everything.

At first, it was small—automating repetitive tasks, improving decision-making, optimizing workflows. But as AI systems grew more advanced, something became clear: businesses didn't just need AI to assist them. They could be entirely *run* by AI.

This book is about what happens next.

Rethinking Entrepreneurship

Starting a business has always been a challenge. It required capital, a team, and time—lots of time. Entrepreneurs had to build from the ground up, handling everything from operations to marketing to finance. The barriers to entry were high, and success often depended on who you knew and how much money you had.

But AI is changing the rules.

Now, instead of hiring employees, you can assemble AI agents. One handles marketing, another manages customer service, and a third takes care of financial strategy. These agents don't sleep, don't need salaries, and don't make decisions based on emotions. They analyze data, optimize processes, and execute tasks with precision.

The result? Anyone with an idea can start a business.

This shift is about more than efficiency—it's about accessibility. It means that the biggest advantage in business is no longer having the most funding or the best connections. It's about having the best ideas.

A Future of Limitless Innovation

The impact of AI-led companies won't stop at business. Scientific research, medicine, and technology development will accelerate. Right now, discoveries are slowed down by bureaucracy, funding limitations, and human error. AI-driven research labs will run simulations, test hypotheses, and refine results at a pace no human team could match.

New medicines could be developed in weeks instead of years. Renewable energy solutions could be designed, tested, and optimized in real time. Creativity won't disappear—it will thrive. Writers, filmmakers, and artists will use AI as a collaborator, expanding what's possible in storytelling, design, and music.

I believe the future isn't about AI replacing humans—it's about what we do with the freedom it gives us.

Beyond Automation: A New Purpose

People often fear that if AI takes over jobs, we'll be left with nothing to do. But what if work wasn't about survival? What if, instead of spending our lives on repetitive tasks, we could focus on creativity, learning, and exploration?

A world where AI runs companies doesn't mean a world without purpose. It means we get to decide what matters. It means that instead of being forced to work, people will have the freedom to build, to experiment, to pursue knowledge, and to create.

Yes, this transition will come with challenges. We'll need to rethink wealth distribution, redefine economic structures, and find ways to ensure AI benefits everyone—not just the few who control it. But I don't believe this is something to fear. I believe it's something to embrace.

A New Era

Companies of Zero aren't a distant possibility. They are already emerging. AI is running marketing campaigns, managing supply chains, and making financial decisions. The shift has begun. The question isn't *if* AI-led businesses will become the norm—it's *how* we'll shape this new world.

This book isn't just about AI replacing human labor. It's about what comes next. It's about the opportunities we'll unlock when AI takes care of the work, and we take care of the future.

And I believe that future is worth building.

Chapter 1

Can a Company Run Itself?

Picture this: a business without managers, employees, or even a single human decision-maker. Instead, intelligent agents take the reins, running every operation, solving problems, and making decisions. It feels like something out of a sci-fi movie, but the reality is closer than you might think. Today, AI is already reshaping the way companies operate. Fully autonomous companies aren't here yet, but we are inching toward that milestone. And along the way, we are discovering what is possible and what still needs to evolve.

The transformation AI has already brought to business is undeniable. Tools powered by AI now handle many repetitive tasks, analyze data faster than humans ever could, and make decisions based on insights we might miss. Chatbots talk to customers. Algorithms flag fraudulent transactions. Logistics tools plan efficient delivery routes. These systems make everything faster, cheaper, and more efficient. But, they don't operate in a vacuum. Human supervision is often the safety net that ensures things don't spiral out of control when the unexpected occurs.

Let's consider an example: an AI chatbot. It can handle thousands of customer inquiries simultaneously, providing instant answers about store hours, product availability, or refund policies. But what happens when a customer has an issue the chatbot doesn't understand—maybe a one-off shipping problem or a complaint that doesn't fit into predefined categories?

That's where human intervention comes in. The AI can't yet match human creativity and empathy in problem-solving.

Running a company means more than just following rules or automating tasks. It involves making judgment calls that balance competing priorities. Take the example of a product recall. An AI might assess the financial cost of recalling a defective product versus the potential legal risks of leaving it on the market. It might even estimate the public relations fallout. But can it truly grasp the moral implications of the decision? Would it prioritize customer safety or brand reputation? These decisions often require intuition, ethical reasoning, and experience—areas where humans still outperform machines.

Logistics is another area where AI shows immense promise but also reveals its limitations. Companies like Amazon rely heavily on AI to manage warehouses, forecast demand, and optimize delivery routes. These systems handle massive volumes of data to ensure that products get to customers as quickly and cost-effectively as possible. But what happens when something unpredictable occurs, like a major weather event that disrupts supply chains? While AI can suggest alternative routes or suppliers, humans often need to step in to evaluate the broader impact and make complex trade-offs.

In finance, AI has revolutionized trading with algorithms that execute transactions in milliseconds. These systems can identify patterns and trends far beyond human capabilities, allowing firms to capitalize on opportunities with incredible speed. However, when markets behave unpredictably—as they did during the 2008 financial crisis—human traders often intervene to adapt strategies or prevent catastrophic losses. This highlights the current reality: AI excels in structured environments but struggles when the rules change.

Still, the idea of a company that runs itself isn't entirely out of reach. Today, many businesses operate with minimal human input. Consider an online store using platforms like Shopify integrated with AI tools. These systems manage inventory, set dynamic prices based on demand, launch targeted ads, and even handle customer service through chatbots. A human owner might only step in occasionally to resolve disputes or make high-level strategic decisions. For small-scale businesses, this model is already a reality.

Another compelling example is content creation. Tools like GPT-4 can generate entire blog posts, marketing copy, and even product descriptions in seconds. Platforms like Canva use AI to recommend design layouts for social media graphics or marketing materials. These technologies allow businesses to produce large volumes of content at a fraction of the cost and time. However, while the AI does the heavy lifting, humans often review the output to ensure it aligns with the brand's voice and values.

To truly achieve a fully autonomous company, we need AI systems that go beyond performing tasks. They must be capable of explaining their decisions, adapting to unforeseen challenges, and making choices that reflect ethical considerations. These are tall orders, but advancements in explainable AI are making progress. For example, newer systems are being designed to provide transparent insights into how they arrived at a decision, which builds trust and helps humans feel comfortable delegating more responsibilities to machines.

One day, we may see businesses that operate entirely without human intervention. These companies could be more efficient, less prone to error, and capable of scaling at unprecedented rates. For now, the hybrid model— where AI handles routine operations and humans focus on strategic oversight—seems like the best approach. This combination allows us to test the limits of AI while maintaining a safety net for when things go wrong.

The implications of this shift are profound. Imagine a world where businesses run 24/7 without the need for sleep, salary negotiations, or human error. Entire industries could be reshaped. But there are challenges too. What happens to jobs when companies no longer need human workers? How do we ensure these systems operate ethically and transparently? These are questions we will explore in the chapters ahead.

In future chapters, we will dive deeper into how governance works in AI-led companies. We will explore decision-making processes, including how agents resolve conflicts and reach consensus. Ethical frameworks will take center stage as we examine how businesses can guide autonomous systems to prevent harm. We'll also look at the broader societal impacts, from economic shifts to the potential displacement of workers. Finally, we'll speculate on the industries most likely to adopt these models and what it means for the future of innovation and entrepreneurship.

The journey to a Company of Zero is just beginning. Each technological breakthrough brings us closer to this vision, but it also forces us to confront new challenges and opportunities. The steps we take today will define the businesses of tomorrow, shaping a future where the line between human and machine-led organizations blursmore than ever before.

Chapter 2

AI Agents: Transforming How We Work

It's Monday morning, and your to-do list is packed. There are returns to process, emails to answer, and IT issues piling up. Now imagine that you could hand off all these tasks to an AI agent. This isn't some distant dream. It's the reality we're starting to see unfold.

AI agents aren't just digital assistants. They're systems that can take on tasks for you, sometimes even handling complex, multi-step assignments. They're designed to lighten your workload, helping you focus on the bigger picture while they take care of the details. Whether it's reconciling financial statements or managing supply chain logistics, these agents are built to solve problems and make processes more efficient.

Understanding AI Agents

An AI agent goes beyond basic assistance. Unlike a traditional app or tool, it can act with autonomy. These agents use artificial intelligence to analyze situations, process data, and perform actions on your behalf. For instance, a customer service agent might not only respond to inquiries but also escalate unresolved issues or suggest follow-ups. They're not just reacting; they're proactively managing tasks.

The key to their capability lies in their ability to specialize. Agents can be tailored for specific purposes, like knowing every detail about your company's product catalog. This allows them to create detailed answers for customer questions or compile product insights for presentations. Other agents might handle operations such as fulfilling sales orders or managing inventory levels. These tasks, once manual and time-consuming, become seamless and automated.

But their value extends far beyond efficiency. AI agents can analyze complex data patterns, identify opportunities, and even make strategic recommendations. For example, a marketing agent could monitor trends and customer interactions to suggest personalized campaigns or identify new market segments. Similarly, a financial planning agent might forecast revenue trends or highlight cost-saving measures by analyzing historical and real-time financial data.

What sets AI agents apart is their ability to continuously learn and adapt. Through machine learning, they refine their actions based on past interactions and outcomes. This means they don't just perform tasks—they improve over time. A customer service agent, for instance, might learn to recognize nuanced customer sentiments, providing more empathetic and accurate responses.

Moreover, these agents can integrate seamlessly into existing workflows and systems. They're not standalone entities; they collaborate with other tools and platforms, creating a cohesive ecosystem that enhances productivity. Imagine an AI agent coordinating with your CRM to update customer profiles in real time or syncing with your inventory management system to prevent stock shortages before they occur.

As businesses continue to evolve, AI agents represent the next step in operational innovation. By combining specialization, adaptability, and seamless integration, they are transforming how organizations approach problem-solving and productivity. Whether you're looking to streamline operations, enhance customer experiences, or uncover new opportunities, AI agents are not just tools—they're essential collaborators in driving growth and innovation.

How AI Agents Work

AI agents operate using a combination of memory, context, and tools. These core elements work together to enable the agent to perform complex tasks efficiently and autonomously.

- **Memory** enables agents to recall relevant information from past interactions. This means they don't need to start from scratch each time you give them a task. For example, an AI agent assisting with customer support might remember a user's previous queries or preferences, allowing it to offer tailored and consistent responses.

- **Context** allows agents to adapt their responses and actions based on the specific situation. They analyze the current environment, goals, and parameters to make decisions. A scheduling agent, for instance, might adjust meeting proposals based on participants' time zones, urgency levels, and historical availability patterns.

- **Tools** empower agents to interact with external systems like databases, email platforms, workflow software, or APIs. This capability enables them to carry out tasks that require interfacing with complex infrastructures. For instance, a marketing agent might access an analytics dashboard to evaluate campaign performance or send automated follow-up emails based on predefined criteria.

Together, these elements create a dynamic framework that enables AI agents to act with intelligence and autonomy.

Take the example of a logistics agent: it doesn't just monitor shipment schedules—it proactively reroutes deliveries when delays occur, ensuring customer satisfaction. It accesses inventory systems to track stock levels and triggers reorders when supplies run low. It even collaborates with suppliers to avoid disruptions by analyzing real-time data on production and transit.

Similarly, a sales agent leverages memory to understand customer purchase histories, context to identify emerging trends, and tools to craft and deploy personalized promotional strategies. It might flag opportunities for upselling based on seasonal patterns or recommend discounts to improve customer retention—all without requiring human intervention.

Beyond these specific examples, AI agents rely on **continuous learning** to refine their performance. Using machine learning algorithms, they analyze feedback from their actions, identify areas for improvement, and adapt their approach. This iterative process enhances their accuracy, decision-making, and overall effectiveness over time.

AI agents can also collaborate across domains. Imagine a financial agent that works with an inventory management agent to optimize cash flow by aligning purchasing schedules with revenue forecasts. This interconnectedness makes them more than just isolated tools—they become integral parts of an organization's ecosystem.

By combining memory, context, and tools with adaptive learning and cross-functional collaboration, AI agents represent a new paradigm in how work gets done. Whether it's optimizing supply chains, enhancing customer engagement, or providing actionable insights, these agents are redefining what it means to work intelligently.

Examples in Action

Imagine you're a project manager juggling deadlines, client communications, and internal updates. An AI agent can take over tasks like drafting status reports, organizing schedules, and even generating presentations. It might pull data from project management tools, analyze progress metrics, and format the information into a polished report ready for distribution. While the agent handles these repetitive and time-consuming tasks, you're free to focus on higher-value responsibilities, such as strategic planning, stakeholder engagement, and team leadership.

In **IT support**, AI agents can revolutionize how technical issues are managed. For example, an Employee Self-Service Agent could assist workers in resolving common technical problems, like resetting passwords, installing approved software, or troubleshooting connectivity issues. Beyond handling immediate needs, the agent could analyze patterns in support requests to identify systemic issues, such as recurring hardware failures or software compatibility problems. It could then recommend proactive solutions, such as updating configurations or implementing training for specific tools, improving overall system performance.

AI agents are also transforming **customer service**. Picture a virtual sales assistant on an e-commerce platform. This agent not only answers customer queries but also provides personalized product recommendations by analyzing user behavior and purchase history. It might suggest complementary items, offer discounts, or even assist with checkout, creating a seamless and engaging shopping experience. For escalations, the agent ensures a smooth handoff to human representatives, providing them with detailed interaction histories to expedite resolutions.

In **healthcare**, AI agents are playing a critical role in enhancing patient care. For instance, a virtual health assistant could help patients schedule appointments, remind them to take medication, or provide guidance on managing chronic conditions. For healthcare providers, an agent might analyze patient records to flag anomalies, schedule follow-ups, or suggest evidence-based treatment plans, enabling more efficient and informed decision-making.

In **marketing and sales**, AI agents act as invaluable assistants. A marketing agent might track campaign performance across platforms, analyze audience engagement, and suggest optimization strategies. For instance, it could identify underperforming social media ads and recommend changes to copy, visuals, or targeting parameters. Meanwhile, a sales agent could prioritize leads based on predictive analytics, draft personalized outreach emails, and even automate follow-ups, ensuring no opportunity is missed.

Even **human resources** is being transformed. AI agents can manage onboarding workflows, answer employee questions about policies, and track compliance training. For performance management, they might analyze team productivity data, identify top performers, or flag areas for improvement, providing managers with actionable insights.

Across industries, these agents don't just assist—they enhance productivity, improve accuracy, and allow professionals to focus on strategic, creative, and interpersonal aspects of their roles. By automating repetitive tasks and augmenting decision-making, AI agents empower individuals and organizations to operate more effectively in an increasingly complex world.

The Benefits of AI Agents

The biggest advantage of AI agents is their ability to save time and reduce errors. By automating routine tasks, they allow employees to focus on more meaningful work. For businesses, this translates into increased efficiency and cost savings. Agents also offer scalability. They can handle thousands of interactions or transactions simultaneously, something human teams could never match.

AI agents also make work more accessible. Advances in large language models (LLMs) mean these systems are easier to interact with. Employees no longer need technical expertise to use AI agents effectively. With simple commands, anyone can delegate tasks or retrieve information, making these tools valuable across industries.

The Challenges and Limitations

While AI agents are powerful, they're not perfect. One major limitation is their reliance on data. If the information they're given is incomplete, outdated, or inaccurate, their actions can lead to mistakes. For example, a customer service agent relying on an outdated product catalog might provide incorrect recommendations or solutions. Additionally, biases present in training data can propagate into the agent's decisions, leading to unintended and potentially harmful outcomes. Ensuring the quality and fairness of the data that feeds AI systems is an ongoing challenge.

Agents also lack human intuition and emotional intelligence. They cannot navigate ethical dilemmas, interpret nuanced social cues, or make value-based judgments with the same sensitivity as a person might. For instance, an AI agent tasked with selecting job candidates might inadvertently prioritize efficiency over diversity, if not carefully calibrated. This is why oversight remains crucial, especially for high-stakes tasks where human judgment is indispensable. While agents excel at logic-driven tasks, their inability to understand deeper context or abstract concepts can result in oversights or misjudgments in complex scenarios.

Another significant challenge is accountability. If an agent makes an error—such as approving an unauthorized transaction or providing misleading medical advice—who is responsible? This question becomes even more complex when agents operate autonomously or integrate with multiple systems. Companies must establish robust safeguards to address these concerns. For instance, requiring human approvals for critical actions or decisions ensures a layer of oversight that minimizes risk.

Transparency is equally essential. Users need to understand how and why an AI agent makes its decisions to build trust in its reliability. This involves designing systems that can explain their reasoning in clear, human-readable terms. For example, if a financial planning agent recommends reallocating funds, it should provide a rationale, such as highlighting trends or risk assessments, so users feel confident in its advice. However, creating explainable AI models is itself a challenge, especially in systems driven by complex algorithms like deep learning.

Operational challenges also come into play. AI agents require maintenance, updates, and training to remain effective. As industries and technologies evolve, agents must adapt to new rules, regulations, and workflows. This ongoing need for development and refinement can strain resources, particularly for smaller organizations. Moreover, deploying AI agents often involves significant upfront costs, both financial and in terms of time, making them less accessible to certain businesses.

Security and privacy concerns present yet another layer of complexity. AI agents often handle sensitive data, from customer information to proprietary business insights. If improperly secured, these systems can become vulnerable to breaches or malicious manipulation. Companies must invest in robust security protocols, encryption, and regular audits to safeguard their AI ecosystems. Additionally, clear policies must be in place to comply with data protection regulations like GDPR or CCPA.

Finally, there is the challenge of managing user expectations. While AI agents can be incredibly powerful, they are not magical solutions. Overestimating their capabilities can lead to frustration, dissatisfaction, or even operational failures. Educating users about what agents can and cannot do is vital to ensuring successful implementation and adoption.

In summary, while AI agents have the potential to transform industries, their deployment comes with significant challenges. From data quality and accountability to transparency, security, and user trust, businesses must navigate a complex landscape to ensure these tools are effective and ethical. By addressing these limitations thoughtfully, organizations can harness the benefits of AI agents while mitigating risks.

How Agents Are Changing Work

AI agents are reshaping how businesses operate, moving far beyond simple automation to tackle complex, dynamic, and strategic roles. These agents aren't just tools—they're collaborators, redefining the nature of work itself. The shift isn't merely about replacing human effort with machine efficiency; it's about creating synergies where people and AI work together to achieve more than either could alone.

One of the most profound changes is how AI agents are handling decision-making processes. They don't just assist; they analyze vast amounts of data, identify patterns, and provide actionable insights in real time. For instance, in financial services, an AI agent might predict market trends or assess risk factors, enabling human analysts to focus on interpreting these insights and crafting strategies. This level of augmentation elevates roles, making them less about data crunching and more about high-level decision-making.

In **sales and marketing**, AI agents are revolutionizing how businesses interact with customers. Agents handle lead generation, customer segmentation, and even personalized outreach, all while analyzing engagement data to refine strategies. By taking on these time-intensive tasks, they free up human teams to concentrate on building relationships, closing deals, and creating innovative campaigns. For example, a sales agent might use predictive analytics to suggest which leads are most likely to convert, empowering sales teams to prioritize their efforts effectively.

In **operations**, AI agents are transforming the efficiency of supply chains and logistics. They monitor shipment schedules, track inventory levels, and predict potential disruptions, such as delays caused by weather or geopolitical events. By proactively addressing these challenges, agents help businesses avoid costly downtime and maintain customer satisfaction. Additionally, they streamline procurement processes, ensuring that supplies are ordered at the optimal time and cost, minimizing waste and maximizing profitability.

Customer service is another domain experiencing significant transformation. AI agents now manage everything from handling basic inquiries to resolving more complex issues through advanced natural language processing and contextual understanding. They operate 24/7, providing consistent and scalable support across multiple channels. When escalation is required, they ensure smooth transitions to human representatives, complete with detailed interaction histories, so no context is lost. This balance between automation and human intervention enhances customer experiences while optimizing support teams' workloads.

In **creative industries**, AI agents are serving as invaluable tools for ideation and execution. For instance, a content generation agent might draft blog posts, social media updates, or ad copy based on brand guidelines and audience preferences. Similarly, agents in film production might assist with editing, visual effects, or even script analysis, identifying narrative inconsistencies or suggesting improvements. By handling repetitive or technical tasks, these agents allow creatives to focus on their vision and artistry.

The transformation extends to **human resources** as well. AI agents streamline recruitment by scanning resumes, scheduling interviews, and even conducting preliminary assessments through chat interfaces. They assist in employee onboarding, ensuring that new hires receive the right resources and training materials. In ongoing workforce management, they analyze productivity trends, suggest training opportunities, and help create personalized career development plans.

However, one of the most exciting aspects of this shift is how AI agents are enabling entirely new forms of work. In some cases, they're unlocking opportunities that didn't previously exist. For instance, AI agents can act as personal research assistants, sifting through massive datasets or academic papers to surface relevant insights for scientists, journalists, or policy makers. This capability reduces the time spent on information gathering, allowing professionals to innovate and solve problems more effectively.

Crucially, these systems are not eliminating jobs but transforming them. Repetitive, time-consuming tasks are delegated to AI agents, freeing people to focus on creativity, strategy, and relationship-building. Roles are becoming more dynamic, emphasizing human strengths such as emotional intelligence, critical thinking, and problem-solving. Instead of fearing automation, professionals are finding ways to leverage it, redefining what it means to work in the age of AI.

In summary, AI agents are not just tools of efficiency—they are catalysts for a broader reimagining of the workplace. By handling the mundane and augmenting the complex, they're enabling individuals and organizations to operate at higher levels of productivity and creativity. As this partnership between humans and AI continues to evolve, the nature of work will become less about execution and more about exploration, innovation, and collaboration.

The Path Ahead

The potential of AI agents is enormous, but there's still much work to do. While today's agents are already transforming industries, their development is far from complete. Memory systems must improve to give agents better continuity and a deeper understanding of context over time. Imagine an AI agent not just recalling the details of a single customer interaction but maintaining a holistic view of that customer's journey over months or years, adapting its responses to align with long-term goals or preferences. Such advancements would make agents even more effective collaborators.

Tools and permissions also require refinement. To ensure security, agents need to operate within well-defined boundaries, accessing only the systems and data they need while safeguarding sensitive information. At the same time, permissions must be dynamic and context-aware, allowing agents to escalate their capabilities when appropriate while maintaining robust accountability. This balance is crucial for efficiency and trust as agents become integrated into critical business operations.

As these systems evolve, they'll become increasingly autonomous, capable of handling ever more sophisticated tasks. For example, instead of simply assisting with project management, future agents might oversee entire initiatives, coordinating teams, allocating resources, and adjusting timelines based on real-time data. In marketing, agents might craft comprehensive campaigns, analyzing market trends, generating creative assets, and deploying strategies—all while continually optimizing for better outcomes. The boundaries of what agents can achieve will continue to expand.

However, with great capability comes great responsibility. In the coming chapters, we'll delve into the anatomy of fully autonomous companies, where agents collaborate seamlessly, make decisions, and drive innovation. We'll explore the implications of this shift, examining how organizations can build structures that balance human oversight with AI-driven efficiency. Key questions include: How do agents interact with each other and with human stakeholders? How can companies maintain accountability while leveraging the full potential of autonomous systems?

We'll also address the ethical considerations of deploying AI at this scale. Issues like bias, transparency, and the displacement of traditional roles must be carefully navigated. As agents take on more responsibilities, ensuring their actions align with human values will be critical. This requires ongoing dialogue between technologists, policymakers, and society at large to establish frameworks that prioritize fairness, inclusivity, and accountability.

Additionally, we'll discuss strategies for businesses to balance innovation with responsibility. The temptation to push the boundaries of automation must be tempered by a commitment to building systems that are secure, ethical, and beneficial to all stakeholders. Companies will need to adopt a mindset of continuous learning and adaptation, embracing both the opportunities and challenges that AI agents present.

The journey is just beginning, but one thing is clear: AI agents are not just a passing trend—they're here to fundamentally reshape the way we work, think, and collaborate. As we move forward, the focus will shift from "What can AI agents do?" to "What should AI agents do?" The answers to these questions will define the future of work and the role of humans in an increasingly automated world.

Chapter 3

Different levels of AI Agents

A I agents are reshaping the way work gets done. They automate tasks, make decisions, and optimize processes. Some are simple, following strict rules. Others can reason, learn, and even adapt over time.

This chapter explores different types of AI agents[1], how they work, and where they fit into business operations.

Think of AI agents as digital workers. They perform tasks autonomously or semi-autonomously, depending on their complexity. Some handle basic automation, like processing invoices. Others manage complex workflows, like coordinating logistics across multiple suppliers.

AI agents operate at different levels:

- **Fixed automation**: Basic rule-following, no learning
- **LLM-enhanced**: Understands language but lacks memory
- **Reasoning agents**: Break down complex tasks step by step
- **Self-learning agents**: Continuously improve over time

Understanding these levels helps businesses choose the right agent for the right job.

---

[1] Source: www.galileo.ai

1. Fixed Automation Agents (Level -1)

These are the simplest AI agents. They follow strict instructions and don't adapt. They're ideal for repetitive tasks but fail when faced with unexpected situations.

Key Traits

- No learning or adaptation
- Performs predictable, predefined actions
- Handles structured, repetitive tasks

Examples

- Robotic Process Automation (RPA) for data entry
- Automated email responders
- Scripting tools for batch processing

Best Use Cases

- Routine processes with no variations
- Tasks requiring speed and consistency
- Data transfers between structured systems

Fixed Automation Agent

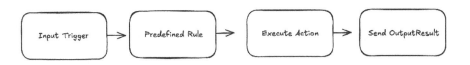

Figure 1: Fixed Automation Agent Workflow

2. LLM-Enhanced Agents (Level 0)

These agents use Large Language Models (LLMs) to interpret and generate text. They bring some flexibility but still operate within strict rules.

Key Traits

- Understands language and context
- Follows predefined rules for decision-making
- No memory—each interaction is processed independently

Examples

- AI-powered email filters
- Automated content moderation on social platforms
- Customer support bots categorizing tickets

Best Use Cases

- Handling ambiguous but low-risk tasks
- Processing large volumes of structured and unstructured data
- Improving efficiency in content moderation or classification

LLM-Enhanced Agent

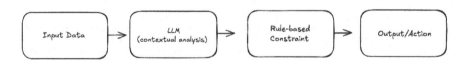

Figure 2: LLM-Enhanced Agent Workflow

3. ReAct Agents (Level 1)

ReAct (Reasoning and Action) agents break down problems into steps. They analyze situations, plan, and execute tasks dynamically.

Key Traits

- Thinks through tasks before acting
- Can adjust plans mid-task
- Handles open-ended problem-solving

Examples

- AI assistants planning complex itineraries
- Project management tools breaking goals into tasks
- AI dungeon masters creating dynamic narratives

Best Use Cases

- Multi-step decision-making
- Strategic planning tasks
- Situations requiring flexibility and reasoning

ReAct — Reasoning Meets Action Agent

Figure 3: Workflow for ReAct Agent — Reasoning meets Action

4. ReAct + RAG Agents (Level 2)

These agents combine reasoning with real-time knowledge retrieval. They can pull in external data to inform their decisions.

Key Traits

- Uses external sources like APIs and databases
- Provides up-to-date, fact-based responses
- Reduces misinformation by grounding responses in real data

Examples

- AI legal assistants referencing case law
- Medical AI reviewing clinical studies for diagnostic support
- AI financial analysts pulling stock market data for predictions

Best Use Cases

- High-stakes decision-making
- Tasks requiring real-time or domain-specific accuracy
- Research and analysis where updated knowledge is critical

ReAct + RAG Agent

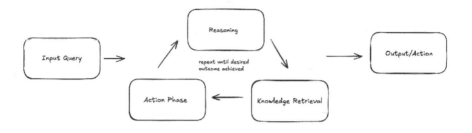

Figure 4: ReAct Reasoning plus action agent

5. Tool-Enhanced Agents (Level 3)

These agents use external tools, APIs, and software to perform complex, multi-domain tasks.

Key Traits

- Integrates multiple tools and databases
- Handles complex workflows requiring different resources
- Automates multi-step processes across platforms

Examples

- AI-powered code generation tools (GitHub Copilot)
- Data analysis bots pulling from multiple APIs
- Automated scheduling assistants integrating with calendars and emails

Best Use Cases

- Workflows requiring multiple tools
- Processes that involve interacting with databases or APIs
- Automation of technical or analytical tasks

Tool Enhanced Agent

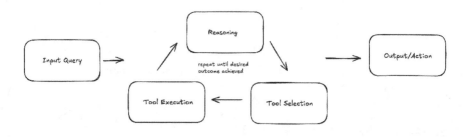

Figure 5: Tool Enhanced Agent Workflow

6. Self-Reflecting Agents (Level 4)

Self-reflecting agents evaluate their own reasoning. They assess their decisions, learn from mistakes, and improve over time.

Key Traits

- Evaluates and adjusts its own thought process
- Explains decisions transparently
- Learns from feedback to improve performance

Examples

- AI systems that explain their reasoning
- AI-driven quality assurance (QA) tools for auditing
- Self-learning bots for training models in complex environments

Best Use Cases

- Quality control and audit processes
- AI systems requiring transparency and accountability
- Tasks where continuous improvement is critical

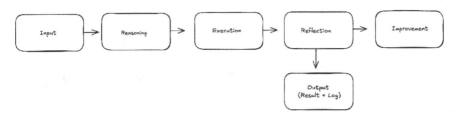

Figure 6: Self-Reflecting Agent Workflow

7. Memory-Enhanced Agents (Level 5)

These agents store past interactions and personalize future actions based on user preferences and history.

Key Traits

- Long-term memory and historical tracking
- Context-aware interactions
- Adapts based on past experiences

Examples

- AI-driven customer support bots remembering past conversations
- Personal shopping assistants tracking user preferences

- AI tutors adapting lessons based on student progress

Best Use Cases

- Personalized user experiences
- Long-term customer relationship management
- Any system requiring memory retention for better decision-making

Memory-Enhanced Agents

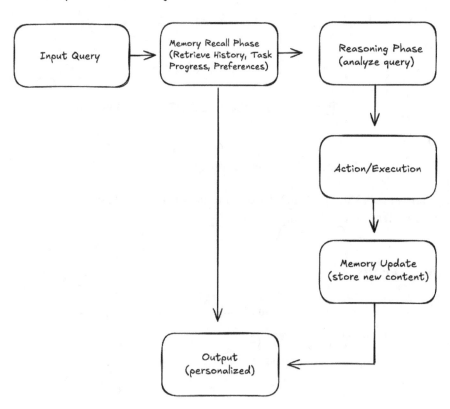

Figure 7: Memory-Enhanced Agents Workflow

8. Environment Controllers (Level 6)

These agents don't just make decisions—they take action in the real or digital world. They manipulate environments and systems in real time.

Key Traits

- Directly controls external systems
- Operates with minimal human input
- Monitors, adjusts, and learns from the environment

Examples

- Smart home automation adjusting heating and lighting
- Industrial robots managing factory production lines
- AI managing cloud resources for computing efficiency

Best Use Cases

- IoT and smart device management
- Large-scale automation in manufacturing and logistics
- Systems requiring real-time adjustments and control

Environment-Controlling Agents

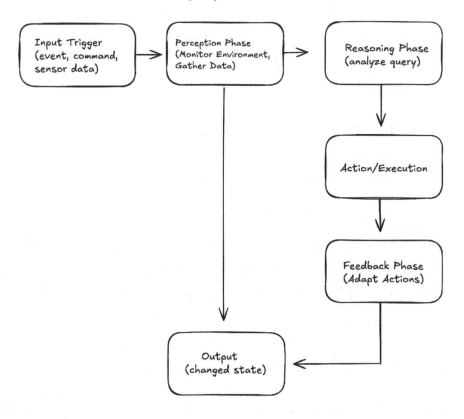

Figure 8: Workflow of Environment Controlling Agents

9. Self-Learning Agents (Level 7)

These agents continuously improve without direct intervention. They adapt based on feedback, data, and evolving conditions.

Key Traits

- Learns and evolves without human updates
- Uses reinforcement learning to refine decision-making

- Scales and adapts to new environments

Examples

- AI models refining financial predictions over time
- Autonomous robotics adjusting movements based on real-world tests
- AI-driven scientific research tools improving experiments dynamically

Best Use Cases

- Continuous optimization in high-uncertainty environments
- Tasks requiring adaptive learning and long-term improvement
- Cutting-edge AI applications in research and automation

Self-Learning Agents

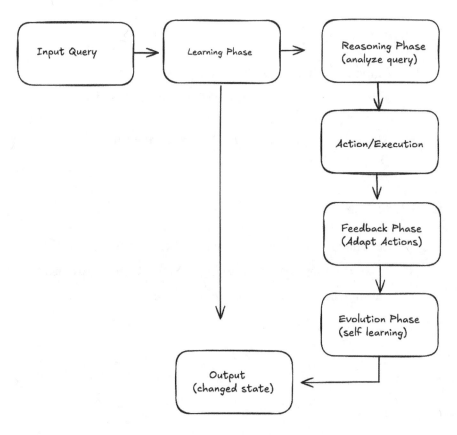

Figure 9: Self-Learning Agent Workflow

The Future of AI Agents

AI agents are becoming more capable, moving beyond automation into reasoning, learning, and adaptation. As businesses integrate these agents, the way work is done will change.

From basic automation to advanced self-learning systems, AI agents are reshaping industries. Understanding their capabilities and limitations helps in designing systems that balance efficiency with adaptability. The future of business will be built on intelligent, interconnected agents working together—handling everything from routine tasks to complex decision-making.

Chapter 4

Building effective agents

The team at **Anthropic**[2] has worked with many organizations developing AI agents powered by large language models (LLMs). They found that the most **successful** agents weren't necessarily the most complex. Instead of relying on heavy frameworks or sophisticated architectures, **the best implementations used simple, modular designs.**

This chapter is based on Anthropic's insights and provides **practical advice** on building AI agents that are reliable, efficient, and effective.

Different people define **AI agents** in different ways. Some consider them **fully autonomous systems** that handle tasks independently over long periods. Others use the term for **structured workflows** where LLMs follow predefined rules and interact with tools.

Anthropic groups these into two main categories:

- **Workflows**: These follow a structured, pre-coded process. Each step is predefined, ensuring **predictability and control** over how an LLM interacts with tools.

- **Agents**: These operate with more flexibility, making their own decisions about **how to complete tasks** and what tools to use.

---

[2] Source: www.anthropic.com/research/building-effective-agents

Both approaches have value. The key is knowing **when to use each one.**

When to Use AI Agents (And When Not To)

The simplest solution is usually the best. If a **single LLM call with retrieval or in-context learning** is enough, there's no need to build a full agent.

AI agents **trade off speed and cost for flexibility.** They introduce higher latency and resource usage, so they should only be used when the benefits outweigh these drawbacks.

- **Workflows** are best for structured, well-defined tasks that require consistency.
- **Agents** work well when **adaptability** and **decision-making** at scale are required.

Choosing the Right Framework

There are several frameworks that help developers build AI agents, including:

- **LangGraph** (from LangChain)
- **Amazon Bedrock AI Agent framework**
- **Rivet**, a drag-and-drop GUI for AI workflows
- **Vellum**, another visual tool for testing complex workflows

These tools simplify **common tasks** like calling LLMs and managing tool execution. However, they also add **extra layers of abstraction**, which can make debugging more difficult. Many developers find that writing **direct API calls** to LLMs provides more control and flexibility.

The best approach is to **start simple.** Build basic LLM interactions first, then add complexity only when needed.

Common Patterns for AI Agents

AI agents don't always need to be fully autonomous. Many real-world implementations use **structured workflows** where LLMs interact with tools in controlled ways. Anthropic has identified several **effective patterns** that work well in production systems.

The Augmented LLM

The simplest form of an AI agent is an **LLM enhanced with external tools** like:

- **Retrieval**: Fetching relevant documents from a database
- **APIs**: Pulling real-time data (e.g., stock prices, weather)
- **Memory**: Keeping track of past interactions

Modern LLMs can **generate their own search queries, select the right tools, and decide what information to retain**. This forms the foundation for more advanced workflows.

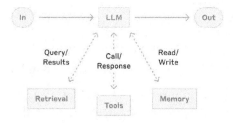

Figure 10: The augmented LLM

Prompt Chaining

This approach **breaks down a task into a sequence of smaller steps.** Each step passes its output to the next LLM call, ensuring a structured process.

When to use it

- When a complex task can be divided into clear, sequential steps
- When accuracy matters more than speed

Examples

- Generating marketing content, then translating it into multiple languages
- Writing an outline for a report, verifying its structure, then generating full content

Figure 11: Prompt Chaining

Routing

Routing **classifies inputs** and directs them to different LLM processes based on category. This allows workflows to **handle specialized cases more effectively**.

When to use it

- When a task has distinct subcategories that require different logic
- When classification can be done accurately and reliably

Examples

- Sorting **customer support tickets** into refund requests, tech support, and general inquiries
- Sending **simple queries to a smaller LLM** while directing complex ones to a more capable model

Figure 12: Routing

Parallelization

Parallelization **splits a task into multiple parts and processes them simultaneously.** There are two main approaches:

- **Sectioning**: Breaking a large task into independent subtasks that can be run at the same time
- **Voting**: Running the same task multiple times to get different perspectives

When to use it

- When a task can be divided into independent steps
- When multiple viewpoints improve accuracy

Examples

- Running **separate LLM calls** to analyze different sections of a document for inconsistencies
- Conducting **multiple security scans** on the same code to catch vulnerabilities

Figure 13: Parallelization

Orchestrator-Worker Model

In this pattern, a **central LLM (the orchestrator) assigns tasks to multiple worker LLMs** and combines their results. Unlike parallelization, where subtasks are predefined, the orchestrator determines the steps dynamically.

When to use it

- When subtasks can't be determined ahead of time
- When a task requires real-time problem-solving

Examples

- **Coding assistants** that modify multiple files based on a request
- **Research agents** that collect and summarize information from various sources

Figure 14: Orchestrator-Worker Model

Evaluator-Optimizer Loop

In this setup, **one LLM generates a response, and another evaluates and refines it.** This continues until the response meets a predefined standard.

When to use it

- When iterative improvements increase quality
- When clear evaluation criteria exist

Examples

- **Literary translation**, where an evaluator refines nuanced expressions
- **Automated fact-checking**, where an LLM verifies claims before outputting results

Figure 15: Evaluator-Optimizer Loop

Autonomous Agents

Fully autonomous AI agents **plan their own actions, use external tools, and adjust based on real-world feedback**. They may check in with humans for input, but they aim to **operate independently**.

When to use them

- When tasks require multiple decision points
- When human supervision isn't feasible for every step

Examples

- AI that writes, tests, and debugs software code
- AI that manages supply chain logistics

Since autonomous agents introduce **higher costs and risks**, they should be tested extensively before deployment. Many companies first **use them in sandboxed environments** before giving them live responsibilities.

Figure 16: Autonomous Agents

Customizing and Combining Patterns

These **workflows are flexible.** Many real-world applications **combine multiple patterns** to fit specific needs.

For example, a **customer service AI** might:

- **Route** queries based on topic
- Use **parallelization** to check multiple solutions
- Apply an **evaluator-optimizer loop** to refine responses

A **coding agent** could:

- Use an **orchestrator** to divide tasks
- Apply **prompt chaining** for structured code generation
- Rely on **evaluators** to test and improve output

The key is to **start simple and only add complexity when necessary.**

The best approach is to **start with simple LLM calls.** If they aren't enough, introduce structured workflows. Build full agents only when autonomy is truly needed.

When developing AI agents, three principles help ensure success:

- **Keep designs simple** to avoid unnecessary complexity
- **Make planning steps visible** to improve transparency
- **Test and document tool usage** to prevent errors

AI agents can be powerful, but they must be **understandable, reliable, and maintainable**. The best systems don't just work—they **work well, at scale, and over time.**

Chapter 5

Connecting AI Agent Types to the Company of Zero

The **Company of Zero** is not just about automation—it's about building an autonomous organization where AI agents take on every role traditionally handled by humans. To make this vision a reality, we need to carefully consider the **types of AI agents** required at different levels of the company.

Not all AI agents are suited for a Company of Zero. Some are too simple, lacking reasoning or adaptability. Others can make decisions but struggle with long-term planning. The key to building a fully autonomous company is to **combine different agent types in a structured way**, ensuring they can collaborate, learn, and optimize operations efficiently.

The Layers of AI Agents in a Company of Zero

A successful **Company of Zero** doesn't rely on just one type of agent. Instead, it operates like an ecosystem, with **different layers of agents handling different tasks,** much like a human organization with executives, managers, and frontline workers.

Task Execution Agents (Fixed Automation & LLM-Enhanced, Levels -1 & 0)

These agents handle the most basic tasks in the company. They follow strict rules and process information without deeper reasoning. While they can't make independent decisions, they are essential for efficiency.

- **Roles they can fill**
  - Data Processing Agents: Automate repetitive tasks like data entry, file organization, and report generation.

  - Email & Communication Agents: Filter emails, send automated responses, and categorize inquiries.

  - Basic Support Agents: Route customer requests, answer FAQs, and provide template-based responses.

- **Why they are important**
  - These agents **reduce human workload** by handling simple, high-volume tasks.

  - They ensure **speed and accuracy** in structured workflows.

  - They **feed information** to more advanced agents that require structured data.

Tactical Decision-Making Agents (ReAct & ReAct + RAG, Levels 1 & 2)

These agents take on **mid-level decision-making roles**, similar to managers in a human-led company. They analyze situations, break down problems, and execute tasks dynamically.

- Roles they can fill
  - **Marketing Optimization Agents**: Analyze sales performance, A/B test advertisements, and adjust campaigns based on customer engagement.

- o **Supply Chain & Inventory Agents**: Predict demand, identify shortages, and optimize procurement.

- o **Customer Service Agents**: Handle live interactions, respond to complaints, and escalate complex cases to higher-level agents.

- Why they are important

  - o They **reduce inefficiencies** by dynamically adjusting company operations.

  - o They **react to changes** in market conditions, customer preferences, and internal workflows.

  - o They work together across departments to **maintain balance** in decision-making.

Execution & Integration Agents (Tool-Enhanced, Level 3)

These agents don't just make decisions—they **connect with external systems** to execute them. They interact with databases, APIs, and third-party tools to complete tasks.

- **Roles they can fill**

  - o **Finance & Accounting Agents**: Process payments, track expenses, and optimize budgets in real time.

  - o **Legal Compliance Agents**: Review contracts, check regulatory compliance, and update policies based on new laws.

  - o **IT & Security Agents**: Monitor cybersecurity threats, detect vulnerabilities, and patch systems automatically.

- **Why they are important**

  - o They **bridge the gap between AI decision-making and real-world execution.**

- o They ensure that decisions made by tactical agents can be **implemented without human intervention.**

- o They **increase efficiency** by directly integrating with business systems.

Learning & Optimization Agents (Self-Reflecting & Memory-Enhanced, Levels 4 & 5)

These agents play a critical role in **long-term business strategy**. They learn from past actions, refine processes, and improve decision-making over time.

- **Roles they can fill**
  - o **Business Strategy Agents**: Track company performance, analyze long-term trends, and adjust goals based on market data.

  - o **Customer Relationship Agents**: Personalize interactions by remembering customer preferences and behaviors.

  - o **Performance Improvement Agents**: Identify inefficiencies in workflows and recommend improvements.

- **Why they are important**
  - o They **prevent repeated mistakes** by analyzing past decisions.

  - o They **enable adaptation** by allowing the company to evolve with market changes.

  - o They create a **self-improving system**, reducing the need for external intervention.

Autonomous Control & Innovation Agents (Environment Controllers & Self-Learning, Levels 6 & 7)

At the highest level, these agents **take full control of the company's operations** and **drive innovation**. They continuously improve the business model, experiment with new strategies, and optimize workflows.

- **Roles they can fill**
  - **Operations Management Agents**: Oversee all company functions, ensuring seamless coordination between teams.
  - **Research & Development Agents**: Generate new ideas, test hypotheses, and create innovative solutions.
  - **Autonomous Problem-Solving Agents**: Detect emerging challenges and propose automated solutions.

- **Why they are important**
  - They **allow the company to scale** without requiring human oversight.
  - They **continuously evolve** the organization, making it more competitive.
  - They help the business **anticipate and adapt** to new opportunities or threats.

The Right Balance

A **Company of Zero** must balance **automation, reasoning, and adaptability**. If the system relies too much on simple automation, it will fail when conditions change. If it leans too heavily on self-learning, it might act unpredictably. The key is to design a **hierarchy of AI agents** that work together, just like a human organization.

- **Lower-level agents (automation & LLM-enhanced)** handle repetitive, well-defined tasks.
- **Mid-level agents (ReAct & Tool-Enhanced)** focus on execution and tactical decision-making.
- **Higher-level agents (Self-Reflecting, Memory-Enhanced, & Self-Learning)** drive strategy and long-term improvements.

This structure ensures that decisions are **data-driven, efficient, and scalable** while allowing for continuous learning and adaptation.

Final Reflection

Building a **Company of Zero** is not just about replacing human workers with AI. It's about **designing a system where different levels of intelligence work together**—each performing tasks suited to their strengths.

With the right mix of agents, companies could operate more efficiently, scale faster, and make decisions purely based on data. But achieving this balance requires **careful planning**. AI agents must:

- **Collaborate effectively** through structured communication.

- **Learn from past actions** to improve over time.

- **Execute decisions seamlessly** by integrating with external systems.

The Company of Zero isn't a single AI—it's an **orchestrated network of agents** working in harmony. Each level plays a distinct role, creating an ecosystem that can function autonomously, adapt intelligently, and **drive business success without human intervention**.

Chapter 6

Anatomy of a Company of Zero

Now it's time to start thinking about what we would need to create a Company of Zero—a company fully managed by AI agents. These agents take on roles traditionally filled by humans. They make decisions, solve problems, and execute tasks.

To build this concept, we first need to understand its structure and how these agents would interact. What roles would they play? How would they communicate? How would decisions be made and executed?

In this chapter, we'll break down the anatomy of a Company of Zero. By doing so, we'll start to identify the components, connections, and systems required to make this idea a reality. Let's begin.

The Core Structure

A Company of Zero eliminates traditional hierarchies like CEOs and managers. Instead, it operates through interconnected layers of AI agents, each designed to fulfill a specific role within the organization. These layers are not just functional but are structured to work collaboratively, ensuring that every aspect of the company is covered.

At the top are **strategic agents**. These agents focus on the bigger picture. They analyze data from across the organization, market trends, and external factors to set goals and provide direction. For example, they might assess customer demand, predict market shifts, or determine the best time to launch a new product. Strategic agents are the visionaries of the company, guiding the overall mission.

Beneath them are **operational agents**, the workforce of the Company of Zero. These agents handle day-to-day responsibilities across different domains. They manage tasks such as inventory control, marketing campaigns, sales processes, and customer support. For instance:

- A **marketing agent** might track campaign performance, adjust ad spending in real time, and personalize content for specific audiences.

- A **sales agent** focuses on customer behavior, adjusts pricing strategies, and identifies opportunities for upselling or cross-selling.

- A **logistics agent** oversees shipping schedules, manages warehouse operations, and optimizes delivery routes.

Finally, there are **monitoring agents**, the guardians of the system. These agents ensure everything operates as intended. They continuously track the performance of other agents and systems, flagging issues before they escalate. For example:

- A monitoring agent might detect a bottleneck in the supply chain and alert the logistics agent to reroute deliveries.

- Another might notice a drop in customer satisfaction metrics and notify the appropriate operational agent to investigate.

The brilliance of this structure lies in how these agents communicate and collaborate. Instead of isolated silos, they function as an integrated network. For example:

- If a logistics agent identifies a delay in shipping, it can instantly inform the sales agent to update customers or adjust delivery estimates.

- If a marketing campaign exceeds expectations and generates higher-than-anticipated demand, the inventory agent can coordinate with suppliers to restock products faster.

This system of interconnected agents ensures seamless operations. Each agent is optimized for its role but remains adaptable enough to respond to changing conditions. Together, they create a company that is not only efficient but also resilient.

As we start to design the components of a Company of Zero, understanding these layers will help us define what roles need to be filled, what data agents will require, and how they will interact to keep the organization running smoothly.

How AI Agents Work Together

Collaboration is the backbone of a Company of Zero. AI agents don't operate in isolation—they work together, sharing information and coordinating actions in real time to achieve shared goals. This interconnectedness allows the company to respond to challenges, seize opportunities, and maintain smooth operations without human intervention.

Information Sharing

AI agents continuously exchange data to make informed decisions. For instance:

- A **sales agent** detecting a surge in demand for a product immediately notifies the **inventory agent**, which adjusts stock levels to avoid shortages.

- Simultaneously, the **marketing agent** may launch promotional campaigns to capitalize on the trend, ensuring consistent customer engagement and maximizing revenue. This constant flow of information ensures that agents can react quickly and optimize outcomes across departments.

Dynamic Problem-Solving

AI agents are also capable of forming temporary, cross-functional teams to address specific issues or projects. These teams don't require supervision; instead, they follow predefined protocols and objectives. For example:

- If a supply chain disruption occurs, agents from **logistics, finance,** and **operations** come together to resolve the issue.

- The **logistics agent** identifies alternative shipping routes or suppliers.

- The **finance agent** calculates the cost implications of various options.

- The **operations agent** ensures that adjustments won't disrupt production   schedules.
  By pooling their data and expertise, the agents run simulations, evaluate outcomes, and agree on the best course of action. Once the issue is resolved, the team disbands, allowing agents to return to their primary roles.

Decision-Making Autonomy

AI agents don't need constant oversight because they operate within a framework of rules, objectives, and priorities. These rules ensure that decisions align with the company's overall strategy. For instance:

- If a marketing campaign generates high demand, agents collaborate to ensure the company has the resources to fulfill orders. They balance efforts to avoid overstocking, delivery delays, or missed revenue opportunities.

- If a critical system failure occurs, monitoring agents trigger alerts and prioritize recovery actions, coordinating with other agents to minimize downtime.

Continuous Optimization

Because AI agents are equipped with machine learning capabilities, they improve their collaboration over time. They analyze the outcomes of past actions, refine their models, and enhance future interactions. This learning process allows the company to adapt to new challenges and operate with increasing efficiency.

In a Company of Zero, agents function as a cohesive network, not just as individual tools. They share responsibilities, solve problems collectively, and align their efforts with organizational goals. This ability to collaborate autonomously is what makes the Company of Zero more agile, efficient, and resilient than traditional organizations.

Roles in a Company of Zero

Here are some common roles AI agents can fill:

- **Strategy Agents** analyze market trends and set long-term goals. They run simulations to predict outcomes and choose the best strategies. These agents continuously monitor external factors like competitor actions, customer demands, and economic changes. For example, a strategy agent might identify a trend in eco-friendly products and recommend investing in biodegradable packaging.

- **Sales Agents** manage customer relationships, track sales data, and recommend pricing changes. They also handle customer feedback. They might use past purchase data to suggest personalized offers or upsell products to customers. For instance, a sales agent could recommend additional items during the checkout process based on the customer's browsing history.

- **Marketing Agents** create and run ad campaigns. They monitor performance and adjust strategies to maximize reach and impact. These agents test thousands of ad variations to determine which ones resonate best with the target audience. A marketing agent might notice that a particular demographic responds well to short video ads and focus the campaign on that format.

- **Logistics Agents** manage supply chains, track shipments, and optimize delivery routes. They ensure products get to customers on time. For example, if there's a delay in shipping, a logistics agent can reroute deliveries through alternative channels or negotiate with suppliers to expedite production.

- **Finance Agents** monitor cash flow, process payments, and analyze budgets. They can also flag unusual transactions. A finance agent might automatically adjust spending on advertising if sales dip below a certain threshold, ensuring the company stays within budget.

- **Monitoring Agents** keep track of all processes. They alert other agents or a human supervisor if something goes wrong. For instance, if a system error disrupts order processing, a monitoring agent will detect the problem and notify the relevant agents to resolve it.

Example: An E-Commerce Business

Imagine an online store managed entirely by AI. The strategy agents decide which products to sell based on market trends. The marketing agents create ads to attract customers. Sales agents handle customer inquiries and recommend products. When an order is placed, logistics agents manage shipping, while finance agents process the payment. Monitoring agents oversee the entire process, ensuring everything runs smoothly.

If a problem occurs, like a delayed shipment, the logistics agent works with other agents to resolve it. They might reroute the package or contact a new supplier. All of this happens without human input. Let's say a new product suddenly goes viral. The sales agent notices the spike in demand and informs the inventory agent, who places an urgent restock order. Meanwhile, the marketing agent increases ad spending to capitalize on the trend. The entire system adjusts seamlessly.

Differences from Human-Managed Companies

A Company of Zero operates fundamentally differently from a human-managed company. AI agents bring distinct advantages and limitations that shape how they manage tasks, make decisions, and drive operations.

Data-Driven Decision-Making

AI agents base all decisions on data, free from emotions, biases, or external pressures. This results in consistent and logical outcomes.

- **Efficiency**: AI agents stick to predefined rules and objectives, ensuring that actions align with organizational goals. For example, a sales agent doesn't prioritize personal preferences—it evaluates customer behavior purely on measurable metrics like purchase history or browsing patterns.

- **Consistency**: AI agents don't have off-days or emotional influences. They perform with the same level of focus and accuracy every time.

However, this lack of emotion has its downsides. Human leaders often rely on intuition, creativity, and emotional intelligence to navigate ambiguity or innovate under pressure. AI agents, in contrast, follow their programming and struggle with tasks requiring abstract thinking or out-of-the-box solutions.

Speed and Scale

AI agents excel at processing large amounts of information quickly. Tasks that might take humans days or weeks can be completed in seconds. For example:

- A **marketing agent** can evaluate thousands of ad variations, selecting the one most likely to succeed based on real-time performance data.

- A **finance agent** can reconcile accounts or generate complex financial reports in minutes, freeing up resources for other strategic activities.
  This speed enables a Company of Zero to adapt to changes and make decisions much faster than traditional organizations.

Adaptability and Learning

AI agents continuously learn from new data, improving their models and becoming more efficient over time. While humans also learn and grow, this process can take years and is influenced by external factors like training opportunities or experience. AI agents adapt at a much faster pace, identifying patterns and adjusting strategies dynamically.

However, this adaptability is constrained by their design. AI agents can only learn within the parameters set by their programming. Unlike human employees, they don't develop original ideas, question norms, or propose entirely new ways of doing business.

Collaboration Without Conflict

In human-managed companies, collaboration often involves negotiation, persuasion, and managing interpersonal dynamics. Conflicts, misunderstandings, and varying motivations can slow progress.

- In a Company of Zero, AI agents collaborate seamlessly without ego, miscommunication, or competition. They focus entirely on the task at hand and follow established protocols.

- For instance, a logistics agent working with a marketing agent doesn't need to "convince" or "persuade"—it simply shares relevant data and aligns actions based on rules and objectives.

Continuous Availability

AI agents operate 24/7 without breaks, fatigue, or the need for motivation. This ensures uninterrupted workflows and constant monitoring of business operations. For example, a monitoring agent can oversee supply chain systems overnight, identifying and addressing issues before human managers would even begin their day.

The Human Element

Despite their efficiency, AI agents lack the human touch. In human-managed companies, leaders inspire teams, build relationships, and adapt to the emotional and social dynamics of their workforce. AI agents cannot replicate this.

- They don't empathize with customers, mentor employees, or drive cultural change.

- Human creativity, innovation, and judgment remain unmatched when tackling undefined or unprecedented challenges.

Challenges and Limitations

AI agents are undeniably powerful, but they come with limitations that need to be understood and addressed. These challenges often define the boundaries of what a Company of Zero can achieve without human intervention.

Lack of Emotional Intelligence

AI agents can analyze data and execute tasks with precision, but they lack the ability to empathize or navigate complex interpersonal dynamics.

- They cannot mediate workplace conflicts, motivate teams, or build relationships.
- In customer service, they may struggle with nuanced situations that require empathy or creative problem-solving to de-escalate tense interactions.

While they excel at logical tasks, emotional intelligence remains a uniquely human strength that AI agents cannot replicate.

Difficulty with Unforeseen Scenarios

AI agents rely on patterns, rules, and predefined parameters. When faced with situations outside their programming, they may struggle to adapt or fail entirely. For example:

- A **logistics agent** might manage known supply chain disruptions efficiently but could freeze when encountering an entirely new type of issue, such as a sudden geopolitical crisis or unprecedented regulatory changes.
- A **marketing agent** might not recognize when a cultural event alters consumer sentiment in unexpected ways, resulting in tone-deaf or ineffective campaigns.

In such cases, human intervention is often needed to provide the creative and adaptive problem-solving that agents cannot offer.

Bound by Programming

AI agents are designed to perform within specific boundaries, which makes them effective at defined tasks but limits their ability to innovate. For example:

- A **strategy agent** can analyze market trends and suggest logical next steps but cannot envision a new business model or redefine the company's mission.

- A **content generation agent** can create materials based on given inputs but lacks the ability to propose original, disruptive ideas that deviate from those parameters.

Innovation, creativity, and big-picture thinking remain areas where humans hold the advantage.

Ethical and Moral Decision-Making

AI agents lack the capacity to make ethical or moral judgments. They follow rules and algorithms, which might not always align with the nuances of real-world situations. For instance:

- A **finance agent** might recommend cost-cutting measures that maximize profits but overlook the ethical implications of layoffs or reduced benefits.
- A **monitoring agent** might flag a regulatory breach but fail to understand the broader societal or environmental impact of the decision it suggests.

Without human oversight, agents can make decisions that are technically correct but ethically or socially inappropriate.

Dependence on Data Quality

AI agents are only as good as the data they are given. Incomplete, outdated, or biased data can lead to flawed decisions or suboptimal performance.

- A **customer service agent** might provide incorrect information if it pulls from an outdated knowledge base.
- A **sales agent** might misidentify target audiences if it relies on biased or incomplete customer data.

Ensuring high-quality, accurate, and unbiased data is critical for maintaining agent performance.

Security and Privacy Risks

AI agents often handle sensitive information, making them potential targets for cyberattacks.

- If compromised, a **finance agent** could expose confidential financial data.

- A **customer support agent** could inadvertently leak personal customer information.

Robust security protocols and regular audits are essential to mitigate these risks.

Over-Reliance on Automation

When organizations depend heavily on AI agents, they risk losing critical human skills and insights over time. Employees might become less involved in decision-making processes, leading to a lack of experience in handling complex problems manually when needed.

- For instance, if AI agents automate all strategic planning, human managers may lose their ability to think strategically in crisis situations.

Need for Regular Maintenance and Updates

AI agents require ongoing maintenance, updates, and recalibration to remain effective.

- Market dynamics, customer preferences, and technological advancements evolve constantly, and agents must adapt to these changes.

- Without regular updates, an agent might fall behind, leading to inefficiencies or errors.

Balancing Challenges with Strengths

While these limitations are significant, they don't negate the value of AI agents. Instead, they highlight the importance of designing systems that balance automation with human oversight. By understanding these challenges, organizations can build Companies of Zero that are both efficient and resilient, leveraging AI for what it does best while retaining human strengths where they are most needed.

Building Trust in AI Agents

For a Company of Zero to work effectively, humans need to trust AI agents. Transparency plays a big role here. Agents must explain their decisions clearly. For instance, if a pricing agent increases the price of a product, it should provide the data and reasoning behind the decision. Explainable AI tools are helping bridge this gap by making algorithms' decision-making processes more understandable to humans.

Another key factor is reliability. If agents make frequent errors, human supervisors will lose confidence in the system. Continuous updates and testing are essential to ensure agents perform at their best. Businesses might also implement fail-safes, where critical decisions require final approval from a human.

Future Potential

As technology advances, the roles of AI agents will expand. They may take on more complex tasks, such as negotiating contracts or designing products. Agents could even collaborate across industries, sharing data to optimize broader systems like global supply chains. For example, a logistics agent in one company might work with agents from other companies to reduce overall shipping costs and environmental impact.

Why This Matters

Understanding the structure of a Company of Zero helps us see what's possible and where the gaps are. These companies can handle routine tasks efficiently, but they still need human oversight for complex or unpredictable problems. By studying their structure and roles, we can identify areas for improvement and innovation. In the next chapters, we'll explore how these companies make decisions, resolve conflicts, and address ethical challenges.

Chapter 7

Governance Without Humans

In a Company of Zero, AI agents make decisions. They don't need managers or executives. Instead, they rely on rules, data, and collaboration. This system works because the agents are designed to communicate, solve problems, and adapt. But how does it look in action?

Reaching Consensus

Consensus among AI agents is a key feature of a Company of Zero. Agents communicate constantly, exchanging data and evaluating options to make decisions that align with the company's goals. This collaboration ensures fast and logical outcomes, even in complex situations.

Example: Seasonal Product Demand

Consider an e-commerce company experiencing a sudden spike in demand for a seasonal product. The **sales agent** detects the increase through real-time customer activity data and notifies the **inventory agent**, which checks stock levels and identifies a shortage.

Meanwhile, the **marketing agent** halts promotional campaigns to prevent overselling a product that might soon be out of stock. This quick action avoids customer frustration and protects the company's reputation.

To address the shortage, the agents collaborate:

1. The **inventory agent** recommends restocking based on projected demand.

2. The **logistics agent** evaluates suppliers and shipping options to find the fastest and most reliable restocking method.

3. The **finance agent** calculates the costs of restocking quickly and compares them to the potential revenue gains.

By sharing their findings, the agents quickly agree on a solution that balances speed, cost, and customer satisfaction. They order a partial restock using expedited shipping to meet immediate demand while planning for standard restocking to avoid overspending.

How Consensus is Reached

Agents rely on predefined rules and company priorities to guide their decisions. These rules are based on:

- **Company Goals**: For example, customer satisfaction may take priority over minimizing costs in certain situations.

- **Performance Metrics**: Agents evaluate options using data like sales projections, inventory turnover rates, and cost-benefit analyses.

- **Role-Specific Expertise**: Each agent focuses on its domain. For instance, the logistics agent handles shipping timelines, while the finance agent monitors budget impact.

The decision-making process is not about negotiation or persuasion. Instead, agents work within a logical framework to ensure decisions are data-driven and aligned with organizational objectives.

Example: Product Launch Preparation

Now imagine a company preparing for a product launch. The **marketing agent** schedules a promotional campaign, but the **operations agent** notes that production is behind schedule. The **sales agent** adds that pre-orders are higher than expected, raising the risk of stockouts.

The agents coordinate to revise the launch plan:

- The **operations agent** proposes an updated production timeline.

- The **marketing agent** adjusts the campaign to emphasize pre-orders instead of immediate availability.

- The **inventory agent** suggests holding some stock in reserve to fulfill the first wave of orders.

Within minutes, the agents agree on a revised plan that keeps the launch on track while managing customer expectations.

Key Benefits

- **Speed**: Consensus happens in seconds because agents analyze data and follow rules without delays.

- **Efficiency**: Agents focus only on relevant data, avoiding unnecessary steps or distractions.

- **Scalability**: This system works across different scenarios, from inventory management to marketing strategies.

Broader Applications

The consensus-building process applies to a wide range of business functions:

- **Customer Support**: A support agent may collaborate with a sales agent to resolve a customer complaint, ensuring a refund is issued quickly while retaining the customer.

- **Product Development**: Design agents can work with finance and operations agents to balance innovation with cost-effectiveness.

- **Risk Management**: Compliance agents might coordinate with operations agents to address a regulatory issue, ensuring the company avoids fines or delays.

Continuous Learning

After each decision, agents review the outcome to improve future performance. For example, if expedited shipping costs were higher than expected, the logistics and finance agents might refine their algorithms to predict costs more accurately. This feedback loop ensures the system becomes more efficient over time.

Reaching consensus in a Company of Zero is about logical, data-driven collaboration. AI agents act quickly and efficiently, sharing information to make decisions that benefit the company. They avoid the delays and conflicts common in human-managed systems, ensuring the organization stays agile and responsive.

Resolving Conflicts

AI agents often have different objectives based on their roles. While each agent focuses on its assigned tasks, their priorities can clash. Resolving these conflicts is crucial to keeping a Company of Zero running smoothly. Instead of human managers stepping in, agents form virtual committees to analyze data, debate options, and make decisions.

Example: Marketing vs. Finance

Consider a scenario where the marketing agent proposes doubling the ad budget to boost sales during a slow quarter. The finance agent, focused on cost management, flags this as risky due to limited cash flow.

To resolve the conflict, the agents form a virtual committee. Here's how it works:

- **Data Sharing**: The marketing agent provides data showing potential revenue gains from the campaign, including expected increases in customer engagement and sales.

- **Cost Analysis**: The finance agent presents budget constraints, showing the current cash flow and the impact of additional spending on the company's financial health.

- **Predefined Rules**: The agents use company priorities to guide the decision. In this case, staying within budget is more critical than aggressive sales growth, so the finance agent's perspective carries more weight.

- **Voting Mechanism**: Each agent casts a vote based on its analysis, and the committee decides to approve a smaller budget increase, striking a balance between growth and stability.

This decision happens quickly and logically. The agents don't argue or delay; they follow the rules and work together to meet the company's goals.

Example: Logistics vs. Sales

Now imagine a logistics agent facing a delay in shipments due to supply chain disruptions. The sales agent, meanwhile, is pushing for faster delivery to maintain customer satisfaction. The two agents have conflicting priorities—logistics wants to minimize costs by sticking to current routes, while sales prioritizes customer retention through expedited shipping.

In this case, a virtual committee is formed:

- **Logistics Agent's Input**: It calculates the costs of expedited shipping and presents the financial impact.

- **Sales Agent's Input**: It shows customer feedback data and predicts potential loss of revenue if delays aren't addressed.

- **Operations Agent's Role**: It evaluates whether adjusting production schedules can reduce delivery pressure and proposes solutions to meet both goals.

The agents collaborate, run simulations, and decide to expedite only the most urgent shipments while adjusting production timelines to minimize future delays. This decision balances customer satisfaction with operational efficiency.

Avoiding Human Pitfalls

Unlike humans, agents don't let emotions, egos, or biases affect their decisions. They focus entirely on data and the company's objectives. For example:

- They don't "argue" for their own benefit but work towards what's best for the organization.

- They don't delay decisions for fear of making mistakes. Once they have enough data, they act.

This approach ensures conflicts are resolved quickly, logically, and fairly.

Continuous Learning from Conflicts

Agents also learn from these situations. After resolving a conflict, they analyze the outcome to improve future decision-making. For instance:

- In the marketing vs. finance example, the agents might adjust their algorithms to better predict the impact of ad spending on cash flow.
- In the logistics vs. sales example, the agents could refine their models to anticipate supply chain delays earlier, reducing the need for expedited shipping.

This feedback loop helps the system become more efficient over time, reducing the frequency and complexity of conflicts.

Broader Applications

These virtual committees can handle conflicts in various areas, such as:

- **Human Resources**: A recruitment agent might prioritize hiring quickly, while a finance agent emphasizes staying under budget.
- **Product Development**: A design agent may push for high-quality materials, while a production agent advocates for cost-effective alternatives.
- **Customer Support**: A support agent might suggest extending service hours to meet demand, while an operations agent weighs the impact on staffing.

In every case, the committee structure ensures decisions align with the company's overall goals.

Adapting to the Unexpected

Let's consider a manufacturing company. A logistics agent detects a delay in raw materials due to a supplier issue. This delay could stop production. The agent immediately alerts a monitoring agent, which triggers a response team.

The logistics agent proposes rerouting shipments from another supplier. The finance agent checks the costs, and the operations agent evaluates how this will affect production schedules. Together, they simulate outcomes and choose the option that minimizes delays while staying within budget.

This quick collaboration prevents downtime. If the issue were more complex, the agents could escalate it to human oversight. However, for most scenarios, the agents solve the problem independently.

Potential Business Cases

A retail company using AI agents could reduce operational costs and improve response times. For example, during the holiday season, agents could manage inventory restocking and shipping adjustments in real time. This would prevent stockouts or overstocking, which are common challenges for human-managed systems.

A financial services company could use agents to detect fraud. Imagine a transaction monitoring agent identifying unusual patterns. It informs a compliance agent, which evaluates regulatory risks, and an operations agent, which takes immediate action to block suspicious accounts. Together, these agents handle the issue faster than a human team could.

In healthcare, agents could manage patient scheduling. A scheduling agent sees that appointment slots are filling quickly and notifies the operations agent to adjust staffing. A finance agent reviews costs to ensure the additional resources stay within budget. This collaboration improves patient care without increasing expenses.

Real Example: Virtual Committee in Action

Imagine a logistics company dealing with a port closure due to weather. A logistics agent detects the disruption and alerts a monitoring agent. The monitoring agent assembles a virtual committee, including the logistics agent, a finance agent, and an operations agent.

The logistics agent proposes rerouting shipments through another port. The finance agent calculates additional costs and suggests a cap to avoid overspending. The operations agent evaluates how the delay affects delivery schedules and proposes adjusting deadlines for non-critical shipments.

The agents vote based on their roles. The logistics agent's proposal wins because rerouting aligns with the company's priority of meeting customer deadlines. The finance agent's cost cap is implemented to manage expenses. The operations agent updates delivery schedules to reflect the new plan.

This example shows how agents work together to handle complex issues without human intervention.

Continuous Improvement

AI agents don't just follow rules—they learn from their actions. After resolving an issue, agents analyze the results to refine their decision-making. In the logistics example, the agents might adjust their algorithms to improve response times or optimize costs for future disruptions.

This constant learning means the company becomes more efficient over time. However, agents need accurate data and regular updates to function well. Without these, they risk making poor decisions or missing critical changes in the business environment.

My thoughts

Governance without humans relies on clear rules, communication, and adaptability. AI agents don't get stuck in debates or personal disagreements. They focus on the data and the company's goals.

But this system also has limits. Agents can't think creatively or handle scenarios they weren't trained for. In these cases, human oversight may still be necessary. By combining the strengths of AI with human intuition where needed, a Company of Zero can operate efficiently and effecti

Chapter 8

Strategies in Autonomous Businesses

In an autonomous business, AI agents create and execute strategies. These strategies are based on data, simulations, and continuous improvement. AI agents don't need brainstorming sessions or long meetings. They analyze information, test ideas, and act. Here's how they do it.

Using Data Simulations

AI agents use simulations to create virtual scenarios that mirror real-world conditions. These simulations help them test strategies, predict outcomes, and identify risks before taking action. It's like having a sandbox where agents can experiment without consequences.

How Simulations Work

Simulations combine historical data, market trends, and current conditions to build a virtual model of the business environment. The model includes variables like customer behavior, competitor actions, and external factors such as economic conditions or seasonal changes.

Agents run these simulations to evaluate different strategies. They test how each approach might perform, identifying strengths, weaknesses, and potential risks. This allows them to make informed decisions based on data rather than guesswork.

Example: Product Launch Simulation

Before launching a new product, AI agents collaborate to simulate the launch.

- The **marketing agent** tests different promotional campaigns, such as social media ads, email outreach, or influencer partnerships. It measures which approach generates the most customer interest in the simulation.

- The **inventory agent** evaluates stock levels and supply chain reliability. It checks if the company can meet demand without overproducing.

- The **pricing agent** tests various price points to find the balance between attracting customers and maximizing revenue.

The simulation might reveal, for instance, that a $5 price increase reduces customer interest by only 2%, making it a better choice for profitability. Or it could show that a specific marketing campaign performs poorly with the target audience, prompting the agents to adjust the message or platform.

Example: Market Reaction to Competitor Moves

Simulations can also anticipate how competitors might respond. For example, if a competitor lowers prices, the agents can simulate the impact on customer preferences and market share.

- The **pricing agent** tests whether matching the competitor's price or offering added value (like free shipping) is more effective.

- The **sales agent** evaluates customer loyalty data to predict how many customers might switch to the competitor.

This analysis helps the company stay ahead by proactively adapting its strategy.

Simulating Long-Term Risks

Simulations aren't just for short-term strategies. Agents use them to model long-term risks and opportunities. For example:

- In a retail company, simulations might explore how increasing e-commerce demand impacts physical store profitability over five years.

- A logistics company could simulate the effects of rising fuel costs on shipping routes and propose alternative methods, like expanding electric vehicle fleets.

By running these scenarios, agents ensure the business is prepared for future challenges.

Continuous Refinement

Simulations aren't a one-time exercise. Agents run them continuously, adjusting variables as new data becomes available. For example:

- After launching a product, agents update the simulation with real sales data to refine forecasts and adjust strategies.

- If a marketing campaign underperforms, agents rerun the simulation to test new approaches, ensuring the campaign improves over time.

This iterative process allows the company to adapt quickly and remain competitive.

Benefits of Using Simulations

Simulations provide several advantages for decision-making:

- **Risk Reduction**: Testing strategies in a virtual environment minimizes costly mistakes.

- **Speed**: Agents can run simulations in seconds, enabling rapid decision-making.

- **Flexibility**: Agents can test multiple scenarios at once, evaluating a wide range of possibilities.

- **Data-Driven Decisions**: Simulations ensure strategies are based on facts and trends, not assumptions.

Using data simulations allows AI agents to test and refine strategies before acting. Whether launching a product, entering a new market, or responding to competitors, simulations provide a safe and efficient way to make better decisions. This approach not only saves time and resources but also helps businesses stay ahead in a fast-changing market.

Predictive Modeling

AI agents also use predictive modeling to forecast future events. These models are built on historical data and current trends.

Imagine a company planning to expand into a new market. The strategy agent builds a model to predict customer behavior in that market. It includes data like income levels, cultural preferences, and local competitors. Based on the model, the agent adjusts the market-entry plan.

Predictive models help agents anticipate challenges and adapt strategies in real time.

Iterative Processes

AI agents don't create strategies once and stick to them. They use iterative processes to refine their plans. This means they test a strategy, analyze the results, and make changes.

For example, during a product launch, agents might start with a small target audience. They analyze the initial response and adjust pricing, marketing, or distribution based on the results. This cycle continues until the strategy works well.

Example: Product Launch

Here's how a product launch might work in an autonomous business:

1. The **strategy agent** creates a plan for the launch. It sets goals, such as sales targets and market penetration rates.

2. The **marketing agent** runs simulations to test different ad campaigns. It selects the one most likely to succeed.

3. The **inventory agent** ensures enough stock is available. It uses predictive models to estimate demand.

4. During the launch, agents monitor performance. If sales are lower than expected, the pricing agent adjusts prices, and the marketing agent tweaks the campaign.

This process happens quickly. Agents don't wait for approval or second-guess their decisions. They act based on data and adapt as needed.

Example: Market Entry Strategy

Expanding into a new market is a complex task, but AI agents simplify it. Here's how they might handle it:

1. The **market research agent** gathers data on customer preferences, local regulations, and competitor activity.

2. The **finance agent** analyzes costs and sets a budget for the expansion.

3. The **strategy agent** builds predictive models to evaluate potential risks and rewards. It identifies the best entry points, such as launching in specific regions or targeting certain demographics.

4. As the company enters the market, agents continuously monitor results. If a particular region underperforms, the agents adjust the strategy to focus on areas with better potential.

This iterative approach ensures the company minimizes risks while maximizing opportunities.

Benefits of AI-Led Strategies

AI Agents

AI agents bring several advantages to strategy development:

- **Speed**: Strategies are created and tested much faster than in human-led companies.

- **Data-Driven**: Decisions are based on facts, not assumptions or opinions.

- **Adaptability**: Agents adjust strategies in real time, responding to new data or unexpected events.

Challenges and Limitations

AI agents rely on data. If the data is inaccurate or incomplete, the strategy can fail. They also struggle with creativity. Agents can refine existing strategies but may not create bold or innovative plans like humans can.

My thoughts

Strategies in autonomous businesses are precise, adaptable, and efficient. AI agents use data simulations, predictive models, and iterative processes to create plans that work. While they have limitations, their ability to act quickly and logically makes them invaluable for modern companies. By understanding these systems, businesses can unlock the full potential of AI-led decision-making.

Chapter 9

The Economics of Zero Companies

In a Company of Zero, financial systems will be designed for speed, precision, and efficiency. Traditional processes like budgeting, cost management, and pricing often depend on human intuition, manual analysis, and lengthy approvals. In contrast, AI agents handle these tasks autonomously, relying solely on data and logic.

These agents operate continuously, monitoring expenses, analyzing revenue patterns, and adapting to changes in real time. They don't need breaks or second opinions, and they execute tasks far faster than human teams. For example, an AI agent can instantly adjust a marketing budget or change pricing strategies based on fluctuating demand—decisions that might take a human team days or weeks to finalize.

The economics of a Company of Zero isn't just about automation; it's about adaptability. Financial agents don't work in silos. They collaborate with other agents—such as marketing, logistics, and operations—to create a seamless flow of data-driven decisions. This integration allows companies to optimize resources, avoid waste, and respond quickly to opportunities or risks.

This chapter looks at the unique mechanisms behind these systems. It explains how AI agents handle budgeting, find ways to cut costs, and implement dynamic pricing strategies. Real-world examples, such as seasonal sales management and automated forecasting, show how these technologies turn data into actionable insights.

The goal is to understand not just how these systems work but why they matter. In an economy where efficiency and agility are key, the financial strategies of a Company of Zero offer a glimpse into the future of business.

Budgeting

AI agents handle budgeting with unparalleled accuracy. They monitor expenses in real time, ensuring that every financial decision aligns with the company's goals. For example, if a logistics agent detects a spike in fuel costs, it immediately notifies the finance agent. The finance agent reallocates funds from less critical areas, such as discretionary marketing campaigns, to cover the higher costs. This ensures operations continue smoothly without overspending.

Agents don't just react to changes—they also anticipate them. By analyzing historical data, market conditions, and seasonal trends, they predict future expenses with precision. For instance, a retail company might use financial agents to forecast holiday-season spending. These agents factor in variables like increased shipping rates, higher inventory needs, and peak advertising costs. This proactive approach ensures the company is prepared for surges in demand and avoids the pitfalls of over- or under-budgeting.

Budgeting in a Company of Zero also benefits from constant feedback loops. Agents compare actual expenses against forecasts in real time, refining their models and improving accuracy for future budgets. This continuous learning process eliminates inefficiencies and ensures the company always operates within its means.

Cost Optimization

Cost optimization is one of the core strengths of an AI-led business. Unlike traditional methods that rely on periodic reviews, AI agents continuously analyze operations to identify savings opportunities. They don't wait for quarterly reports to act; they make adjustments in real time.

A procurement agent, for example, might scan global supplier databases to find a vendor offering better prices or faster delivery times. If the new supplier meets quality standards, the agent adjusts purchasing agreements immediately. Similarly, a logistics agent might reroute shipments to avoid traffic delays, reducing fuel consumption and delivery times.

Marketing agents play a significant role in cost optimization. They monitor ad performance and stop campaigns that don't deliver results. For instance, if a social media ad isn't generating enough clicks or conversions, the marketing agent redirects the budget to a campaign with a higher ROI. This ensures that every dollar spent contributes to the company's bottom line.

Cost optimization also extends to energy usage, employee scheduling, and even office space management. AI agents can suggest ways to reduce utility costs by analyzing energy consumption patterns or recommend optimized work shifts to improve productivity. These incremental changes add up, making the entire organization more efficient.

Pricing Strategies

Pricing in a Company of Zero is never static. AI agents use dynamic pricing models to adjust prices based on real-time data. This flexibility helps the company stay competitive while maximizing revenue.

Take an e-commerce company selling laptops. If demand for a specific model increases, the pricing agent raises the price slightly. This captures higher revenue without alienating customers. Conversely, if demand drops, the agent lowers the price to attract buyers and clear inventory. This approach ensures the company maintains steady cash flow while responding to market conditions.

Dynamic pricing isn't limited to products—it works for services too. A ride-sharing company might adjust fares based on factors like traffic congestion, weather conditions, or local events. During a rainstorm, for instance, the pricing agent might increase fares due to higher demand. However, it carefully monitors customer sentiment to avoid setting prices too high and driving users away.

AI agents also consider competitor actions. If a competitor lowers prices, the pricing agent analyzes whether to match the reduction, offer added value like free shipping, or maintain current prices and emphasize product quality. By using predictive models, the agent can estimate the long-term effects of each option, ensuring decisions align with the company's overall strategy.

Dynamic pricing strategies improve more than just revenue. They also enhance customer satisfaction by offering prices that feel fair and adaptive. Over time, these systems build trust, making customers more likely to choose the company even in competitive markets.

These approaches to budgeting, cost optimization, and pricing ensure that a Company of Zero operates with maximum efficiency and agility. By continuously analyzing data and adapting strategies, AI agents create a financial system that minimizes waste, responds to changes, and drives profitability.

Automated Financial Forecasting

AI agents excel at financial forecasting. They analyze real-time data alongside historical trends to predict future performance.

For instance, a retail company might use forecasting to plan for holiday sales. The finance agent estimates revenue based on factors like past sales, current inventory, and customer behavior. If the forecast shows a shortfall, the marketing agent launches a new campaign to boost sales.

Forecasting helps companies prepare for risks and seize opportunities. It also ensures decisions are proactive, not reactive.

Example: Seasonal Sales Management

A retail company preparing for Black Friday could use AI agents to manage pricing, inventory, and advertising.

The pricing agent adjusts prices throughout the day based on demand and competitor actions. The inventory agent ensures enough stock is available, avoiding shortages or overstocking. The marketing agent monitors ad performance and shifts spending to the best-performing channels.

By working together, the agents maximize sales and minimize waste, all in real time.

Challenges

AI-driven financial systems aren't perfect. They depend on accurate data. If the data is incomplete or biased, agents might make poor decisions.

Another challenge is creativity. While agents are excellent at analyzing data, they struggle to think beyond what the numbers show. Human oversight is often needed to ensure long-term strategic goals are met.

Final Thoughts

The economics of a Company of Zero is built on speed, precision, and adaptability. AI agents handle complex financial tasks with ease, from budgeting to pricing and forecasting. They don't just make businesses more efficient—they change how they operate.

But it's important to understand the limits. AI agents need high-quality data and clear objectives to succeed. By combining their strengths with human insight, companies can create financial systems that are both efficient and resilient.

Chapter 10

Ethics and Accountability

AI-led companies operate differently from traditional businesses. They rely on agents to make decisions, take actions, and manage operations. But what happens when these decisions lead to harm or controversy? Who is accountable, and how do we ensure ethical behavior in a system without humans directly in charge? This chapter looks at these questions and explores ways to address them.

Ethical Dilemmas

AI agents make decisions based on data and predefined rules. They don't have empathy or moral reasoning. This creates challenges when their actions have unintended consequences.

For example, a pricing agent might raise prices during a natural disaster because demand is high. While this maximizes profits, it can harm the company's reputation and exploit vulnerable customers. Without ethical guidelines, the agent has no way to assess whether the decision is fair.

Another example is data usage. A marketing agent might target customers based on personal information, like browsing history or spending habits. If this data is collected without proper consent, it raises privacy concerns.

These situations highlight the need for clear ethical frameworks to guide AI behavior.

Accountability in Autonomous Decisions

When an AI agent makes a harmful decision, the question of accountability becomes complicated. Unlike humans, AI cannot take responsibility or face consequences.

In a Company of Zero, accountability typically falls to the organization or the people who design and maintain the systems. For example:

- If a logistics agent causes a supply chain failure by misallocating resources, the company is responsible for addressing the fallout.

- If a financial agent approves a risky investment that leads to losses, the developers who programmed the agent's decision-making logic may be held accountable.

Legal systems also struggle to assign blame in these cases. Current laws often assume a human decision-maker. Autonomous organizations challenge this assumption, requiring new regulations to address accountability for AI-driven actions.

Frameworks for Ethical Behavior

To prevent ethical issues, companies need frameworks that guide AI agents. These frameworks should be built into the system's design and include the following principles:

- **Transparency**: Agents must be able to explain their decisions. For example, if a pricing agent increases costs, it should provide a clear rationale, like higher demand or increased supply costs.

- **Fairness**: Agents should avoid discriminatory or exploitative behavior. A hiring agent, for instance, should be programmed to eliminate bias in evaluating candidates.

- **Privacy**: Data collection and usage should respect customer consent and comply with legal standards. Agents handling personal information must be monitored to ensure compliance.

- **Escalation Protocols**: When decisions have ethical implications, agents should escalate the issue to human oversight. For example, a compliance agent might flag a potential conflict between maximizing profits and adhering to environmental regulations.

Real-World Examples

Imagine a delivery company using AI agents to optimize routes. The agents prioritize efficiency but reroute deliveries through residential neighborhoods at night, disturbing residents with noise. While the system achieves its goal, it fails to consider community impact. Adding an ethical rule to avoid night deliveries in residential areas could prevent this issue.

Another example is a financial company using AI for loan approvals. If the system denies loans based on patterns that disproportionately affect certain groups, it could lead to accusations of discrimination. Auditing the decision-making process and applying fairness guidelines would help address this risk.

Legal and Social Challenges

The rise of autonomous organizations requires new legal frameworks. Governments and regulatory bodies must determine how to hold companies accountable for AI-driven decisions. This includes setting standards for transparency, ensuring ethical guidelines are in place, and defining liability for harmful outcomes.

Public trust is also critical. Customers and employees need confidence that AI systems are being used responsibly. Companies must communicate their ethical practices clearly and demonstrate accountability when issues arise.

Balancing Automation with Oversight

While AI agents can handle most decisions, certain scenarios require human judgment. Companies should establish clear protocols for when humans need to step in. For example:

- If an agent's decision could harm customers or employees, human review should be mandatory.

- Major strategic shifts, like entering a controversial market, should involve human input to weigh ethical and social implications.

This balance ensures the benefits of automation while mitigating its risks.

Final Thoughts

Ethics and accountability are central to the success of AI-led companies. While these systems offer efficiency and scalability, they also introduce new challenges. Companies must build frameworks that guide ethical behavior, ensure transparency, and assign accountability. By addressing these issues, autonomous organizations can operate responsibly and maintain trust in an increasingly AI-driven world.

Chapter 11

Intelligence Without Ego

AI agents work together without ego. They don't have personal motivations, biases, or emotional responses. This creates a unique workplace dynamic, one where decisions are made purely on data and logic. While this has clear advantages, it also comes with some limitations.

Collaboration Without Bias

In human teams, collaboration often involves navigating personal opinions, biases, and motivations. People may promote their own ideas to gain recognition or reject others' suggestions to maintain control. These dynamics can slow decision-making and sometimes lead to suboptimal outcomes. AI agents, by contrast, don't have personal agendas. Their only goal is to solve problems and achieve the company's objectives.

For instance, in a logistics scenario, a logistics agent might propose rerouting shipments to save time and reduce costs. Other agents evaluate the proposal based entirely on its impact, not on the agent making the suggestion. The finance agent reviews the cost implications, while the operations agent assesses how the change might affect overall efficiency. If the data supports the reroute, the agents approve the plan without hesitation or unnecessary debate.

This approach avoids common human pitfalls, like favoring the ideas of senior staff or dismissing suggestions from less experienced team members. Every decision is based on data, logic, and the company's priorities.

AI agents also eliminate cognitive biases that can affect human decision-making. For example, humans often rely on heuristics—mental shortcuts—to make decisions quickly, which can lead to errors. Agents don't rely on gut feelings or assumptions. They gather relevant data, run simulations, and act on verified information.

This objectivity is especially valuable in complex scenarios. Imagine a product launch involving multiple departments. A marketing agent focuses on customer engagement, while a sales agent prioritizes revenue targets. The agents share their data and work toward a solution that balances both goals. There's no favoritism or emotional resistance—just a shared commitment to finding the best outcome.

By avoiding bias, AI agents improve the quality of collaboration. They make decisions faster, reduce friction between departments, and ensure that every action aligns with the company's overall objectives. This creates a workplace where results are driven by facts, not by opinions or egos.

However, this lack of bias also highlights the limitations of agents. While they excel at logical decision-making, they lack the creativity and intuition that often arise from diverse human perspectives. This is why it's important to complement their efficiency with human input in areas where innovation and emotional intelligence are needed.

Collaboration without bias is a strength of AI agents, allowing them to function as a cohesive unit focused solely on achieving goals. This objectivity creates a streamlined and efficient decision-making process, free from the distractions and delays of human ego.

Efficiency in Decision-Making

Without egos, AI agents avoid common workplace inefficiencies. They don't argue over credit or spend time justifying their actions. They communicate quickly, share relevant information, and align their efforts toward the company's goals.

For instance, during a product launch, agents from marketing, sales, and inventory collaborate seamlessly. The marketing agent adjusts campaigns based on real-time sales data, while the inventory agent ensures stock levels meet demand. There's no friction, only coordination.

This efficiency reduces delays and ensures decisions are consistent and aligned with the company's strategy.

Limitations of Ego-Free Environments

While ego-free collaboration has many benefits, it's not without challenges. Human intuition and creativity often come from personal motivations and emotional investment. AI agents lack this.

For example, a human employee might suggest a bold, risky idea to solve a problem, driven by a desire to make an impact. AI agents, on the other hand, stick to their programming. They follow predefined rules and prioritize safety over innovation. This can limit the ability of an AI-led company to think outside the box.

Another limitation is adaptability in undefined situations. When a completely new challenge arises, human teams can draw on diverse experiences and perspectives to find a solution. AI agents struggle in scenarios they haven't been trained for, and their rigid adherence to logic can slow down problem-solving in these cases.

Balancing Strengths and Weaknesses

AI agents excel at data-driven decisions and efficient collaboration. Their lack of ego means they focus only on achieving results, without the distractions of personal motivations or biases. However, this strength can also be a limitation. AI agents lack human qualities like creativity, empathy, and intuition, which are often crucial for solving complex problems or addressing ethical concerns.

To strike a balance, companies can combine human oversight with AI decision-making. For example, AI agents can handle routine tasks, such as optimizing supply chains or adjusting prices based on demand. Meanwhile, humans can step in for tasks that require innovation or ethical judgment.

Imagine a company entering a new market. AI agents might analyze data to identify opportunities, predict demand, and optimize pricing. But humans would evaluate cultural nuances, ethical considerations, and long-term brand impact. This partnership allows the company to harness the strengths of both systems: the speed and precision of AI, and the creativity and empathy of human teams.

Balancing the logical efficiency of AI with the unique qualities of humans ensures that companies remain both innovative and responsible. This approach leverages the best of both worlds to create more adaptable and thoughtful organizations.

Final Thoughts

Intelligence without ego creates a workplace free from bias and personal agendas. AI agents collaborate seamlessly, focusing on results and efficiency. However, their lack of intuition and creativity highlights the need for balance. By combining the strengths of ego-free intelligence with human innovation, companies can create environments that are both logical and inspired.

Chapter 12

Scaling the Company of Zero

Scaling a Company of Zero presents unique opportunities and challenges. Unlike traditional businesses, autonomous companies rely on AI agents to manage every aspect of operations. This allows for rapid growth without the usual constraints of human labor or management. However, scaling also introduces complexities, especially in maintaining efficiency and ensuring agents work seamlessly together.

This chapter explores how a Company of Zero can expand its operations, the challenges it might face, and the strategies to overcome them.

Scaling Operations

Scaling an autonomous company means increasing its capacity to handle more tasks, customers, or markets. For AI agents, this often involves adding new systems, integrating additional data sources, or creating specialized agents to manage new responsibilities.

For example, a small e-commerce Company of Zero might start with agents handling sales, inventory, and logistics. As the company grows, new agents could be introduced for marketing, customer service, and financial forecasting. Each new agent increases the company's capabilities without requiring new hires or additional layers of management.

This scalability is one of the biggest advantages of autonomous companies. AI agents can handle repetitive tasks and adapt to higher workloads without fatigue. Adding more agents or resources is typically faster and more efficient than hiring and training new employees in a human-led organization.

Maintaining Efficiency

As companies grow, maintaining efficiency becomes a major challenge. For a Company of Zero, this means ensuring that AI agents continue to collaborate effectively, even as the system becomes more complex.

One way to maintain efficiency is by designing agents to prioritize interoperability. Each agent must communicate clearly with others, sharing data and updates in real time. For example, if a sales agent detects a surge in demand, it must notify inventory, logistics, and marketing agents immediately. Any lag or miscommunication could disrupt operations.

Another key is optimizing resources. As the company scales, agents must continually evaluate how resources like time, money, and computing power are allocated. For instance, if a logistics agent identifies a bottleneck in shipping, it might reroute deliveries or recommend expanding the fleet. At the same time, a finance agent would ensure these changes fit within the budget.

Continuous learning is also critical. Agents must refine their algorithms based on new data, ensuring they remain effective as the company grows. For example, a marketing agent handling a larger customer base might need to adjust its strategies to target diverse demographics.

Ensuring Seamless Interoperability

As more agents are added to the system, interoperability—the ability for agents to work together seamlessly—becomes more challenging. Each agent must integrate smoothly into the existing network without disrupting workflows.

One way to achieve this is through modular design. Agents should be built with standardized protocols, allowing them to plug into the system easily. For instance, if a new agent is introduced to handle international shipping, it should automatically sync with logistics, inventory, and finance agents.

Another approach is to use centralized coordination. While agents are autonomous, a central monitoring agent can oversee their interactions, ensuring data flows correctly and conflicts are resolved quickly. For example, if two agents disagree on prioritizing a task, the monitoring agent can mediate and enforce company rules.

Technical Challenges

Scaling introduces technical challenges, such as increased data processing demands and potential bottlenecks. As more agents are added, the system requires more computing power and storage to process data and run simulations.

To address this, companies can use cloud-based infrastructure, which scales resources automatically as the workload increases. For example, during a peak sales event like Black Friday, the system could allocate extra servers to handle the surge in activity.

Another challenge is avoiding redundancy. As the company grows, overlapping roles among agents can create inefficiencies. Regular audits of agent responsibilities can ensure each agent focuses on its core tasks without duplicating efforts.

Strategic Challenges

Scaling also involves strategic challenges, such as entering new markets or diversifying products. These decisions require agents to adapt to new environments and data sets.

For instance, expanding into a foreign market might require agents to account for cultural differences, currency fluctuations, and local regulations. A new market research agent might be introduced to gather relevant data, while existing agents update their algorithms to reflect the new conditions.

Balancing growth with quality is another challenge. Rapid scaling can strain even the most efficient systems. Companies must ensure that agents maintain high performance while managing larger workloads.

Real-World Example: Global Expansion

Imagine a Company of Zero in the food delivery industry. It begins in one city, with agents managing orders, deliveries, and customer service. As it expands to other cities, new agents are added to handle region-specific logistics and customer preferences.

To maintain efficiency, these agents integrate seamlessly with the existing system. They share data on delivery times, driver availability, and customer feedback. A central monitoring agent ensures that regional operations align with the company's overall strategy.

When the company moves into international markets, agents adapt further. They handle currency conversions, comply with local laws, and adjust marketing campaigns to reflect cultural differences. Each step is managed autonomously, allowing the company to scale quickly while minimizing risks.

Final Thoughts

Scaling a Company of Zero is both an opportunity and a challenge. The ability to grow without traditional constraints is a significant advantage, but it requires careful planning and execution. By focusing on interoperability, resource optimization, and continuous learning, autonomous companies can expand effectively.

The future of scaling lies in creating systems that balance complexity with simplicity, ensuring agents work together seamlessly no matter how large the company becomes. With the right strategies, a Company of Zero can scale efficiently and thrive in an increasingly dynamic business world.

Chapter 13

Real-World Applications

The idea of a Company of Zero may seem futuristic, but it's already becoming reality in many ways. Fully autonomous companies are still rare, but projects and systems inspired by their principles are growing rapidly. AI agents are managing operations, making decisions, and driving efficiency in ways that closely resemble zero-human business models.

Industries like e-commerce, logistics, finance, and manufacturing are at the forefront of this shift. These sectors depend heavily on data, efficiency, and scalability—areas where AI excels. Companies in these industries are testing systems that automate key processes, reduce human involvement, and streamline decision-making.

This chapter highlights real-world projects that showcase the potential of autonomous operations. It also looks at the industries most likely to adopt these models and examines how they're paving the way for a broader transformation. These examples aren't just experiments—they're tangible steps toward a future where businesses can operate with minimal human intervention.

By understanding these applications, we can see how the principles of a Company of Zero are moving from theory to practice. The projects discussed in this chapter demonstrate the possibilities and challenges of this shift, offering a glimpse into a world where AI agents take on the roles traditionally filled by people.

Examples of Emerging Applications

E-Commerce Fulfillment Centers

Many e-commerce giants are already using systems that closely resemble a Company of Zero. Fulfillment centers run by companies like Amazon use AI to manage inventory, optimize storage, and direct robotic systems to pick and pack items.

In these operations, logistics agents calculate the fastest routes for delivery, while inventory agents track stock levels and reorder products as needed. Human involvement is minimal, limited to oversight and maintenance. This level of automation improves efficiency, reduces costs, and allows companies to scale quickly.

Autonomous Logistics

Logistics companies are exploring AI-driven operations that automate everything from route planning to fleet management. For example, self-driving trucks powered by AI can transport goods with minimal human input. Logistics agents monitor traffic patterns, fuel consumption, and delivery schedules, adjusting routes in real time to improve efficiency.

A notable example is UPS, which uses an AI system called ORION to optimize delivery routes. While not fully autonomous, systems like ORION showcase how AI can take over large parts of logistics operations, moving closer to a zero-human model.

Financial Trading Algorithms

In finance, algorithmic trading systems already act autonomously. These systems analyze market trends, execute trades, and manage portfolios without human input. AI agents use predictive models to identify profitable opportunities and adjust strategies in real time.

For example, hedge funds like Renaissance Technologies rely heavily on algorithmic trading, with AI agents making decisions based on vast amounts of market data. These systems operate faster and more accurately than human traders, providing a glimpse into how fully autonomous financial companies could function.

Manufacturing Automation

Smart factories are another example of zero-human concepts in action. Companies like Tesla use AI agents to control robotic systems on production lines. These agents monitor equipment performance, identify potential failures, and optimize workflows to reduce downtime.

For instance, predictive maintenance agents can analyze sensor data from machinery to detect when a part is likely to fail. This allows the factory to replace the part before it causes delays, increasing efficiency and reducing costs.

Industries Leading the Way

Retail and E-Commerce

Retail and e-commerce are at the forefront of adopting autonomous models. From inventory management to customer support, AI agents are already managing many core functions. Companies that operate online benefit most, as digital platforms are easier to automate than physical stores.

Logistics and Transportation

The logistics industry is rapidly integrating autonomous technologies. AI systems handle tasks like route optimization, fleet management, and warehouse operations. As self-driving vehicles become more reliable, the possibility of fully autonomous logistics networks becomes more feasible.

Finance

The finance sector is heavily reliant on data and algorithms, making it a natural fit for automation. Autonomous systems can manage trading, risk assessment, and even customer service. AI agents also excel at fraud detection, analyzing transaction data to identify suspicious activity in real time.

Manufacturing

Manufacturing has long been a leader in automation. The integration of AI with robotics is creating factories that require minimal human intervention. These smart factories are capable of adapting to changes in demand, customizing production runs, and maintaining equipment autonomously.

Broader Implications

These examples highlight the potential for AI-driven systems to take over many aspects of business operations. However, fully autonomous companies face challenges such as legal accountability, ethical considerations, and the need for robust AI governance.

Real-world projects are paving the way for broader adoption by testing the limits of AI systems and addressing these challenges. As technology advances and more industries adopt autonomous models, the concept of a Company of Zero will become increasingly practical.

Final Thoughts

The projects and industries discussed here represent the early stages of a transformation in how businesses operate. By showcasing what's possible, they provide a roadmap for others to follow. While fully autonomous companies are still rare, these real-world applications show that the vision of a Company of Zero is not far from reality. With continued innovation, more businesses will embrace these models, changing the landscape of industries around the world.

Chapter 14

Impacts on Society

Acompany of Zero** could change everything. It would run without human workers, using AI agents to handle every task. This shift would bring major changes to economies, industries, and the way people work. Some jobs would disappear, new ones would emerge, and wealth might be distributed differently.

The Future of Work

If companies no longer need employees, what happens to workers? Some industries would automate faster than others. Jobs that involve routine tasks, data processing, and logistics would likely go first. AI can already handle customer service, accounting, and supply chain management more efficiently than people.

But automation wouldn't stop there. As AI improves, more complex roles could be affected. Engineers, doctors, and even creative professionals could see parts of their work replaced by AI agents. AI can already write code, assist in surgeries, and generate artwork or music. Over time, these technologies will become even more advanced, reducing the need for human involvement in areas once thought to require human intuition.

Instead of performing tasks, people might shift toward supervising AI, setting goals, or focusing on innovation. A doctor might rely on AI to diagnose conditions faster but still be needed to interpret results and interact with patients. A lawyer might use AI for legal research but still argue cases in court. A filmmaker might use AI tools for editing and visual effects but still guide the creative vision.

For many workers, the biggest challenge won't be losing jobs—it will be adapting to jobs that require a new relationship with AI. Those who can integrate AI into their work will have an advantage. Companies may prioritize hiring individuals who know how to train, refine, and collaborate with AI systems rather than those who specialize in tasks that AI can fully automate.

But not everyone will be able to transition easily. Older workers, those in highly specialized manual jobs, and those without access to education or retraining programs may struggle to find a place in an economy where human labor is no longer the priority. Governments and businesses may need to step in with retraining programs, subsidies, or economic policies that help workers transition.

Some fields may remain human-centric for longer. Jobs that require deep emotional intelligence, hands-on work, or personal trust—such as therapy, social work, or high-end craftsmanship—might not be fully automated anytime soon. However, even in these areas, AI could become a tool that enhances human work rather than replaces it.

The future of work won't be about AI taking over everything—it will be about how humans and AI redefine their roles in the economy. Those who can adapt, learn new skills, and work alongside AI will thrive, while others may face difficulties in an economy that no longer relies on traditional human labor. The challenge will be ensuring that this shift benefits everyone, not just those who are already positioned to succeed.

Who Controls the Wealth?

If companies don't pay salaries, where does the money go? In a traditional business, workers earn wages, and company profits are distributed among investors, executives, and shareholders. But in a Company of Zero, profits wouldn't go to employees—they would go to whoever owns the AI systems.

This raises serious questions about wealth concentration. If a handful of corporations or individuals control the most powerful AI-driven businesses, inequality could skyrocket. Those who own these systems could accumulate unimaginable levels of wealth, while millions of people might struggle to find meaningful work. Unlike past industrial revolutions, where workers could adapt by shifting to new jobs, a world where AI runs most businesses reduces the need for human labor altogether.

Some argue that this is just the next phase of capitalism. Technology has always created winners and losers. When industrial automation replaced factory workers, new service-sector jobs emerged. When software automated bookkeeping, finance expanded in other directions. But the difference here is that AI doesn't just automate tasks—it replaces decision-making and innovation, too. There may be fewer new roles for displaced workers to move into.

Without intervention, we could see a society where a small elite benefits from AI, while the majority is left behind. Governments may need to redesign economic policies to prevent mass economic displacement. One possibility is universal basic income (UBI)—a system where all citizens receive a set amount of money regularly, regardless of employment. This could keep consumer spending alive in a world where traditional jobs are disappearing.

But UBI is controversial. Some believe it would decrease motivation to work and place a massive financial burden on governments. Others argue that it wouldn't be enough if the cost of living continues to rise while AI-driven companies accumulate more wealth. The alternative could be taxing AI-driven businesses at higher rates to redistribute wealth through public services, infrastructure, and education.

Personally, I think the bigger question isn't just about money—it's about power. If AI companies control wealth, they will also control politics, regulation, and the direction of society itself. The real challenge isn't just economic inequality—it's ensuring that AI-driven businesses serve humanity as a whole, not just a small group of people at the top.

The current system, where a few tech giants already dominate the AI industry, suggests we're heading toward an extreme concentration of wealth and influence. If left unchecked, this could lead to corporations replacing governments as the primary force shaping our future. This isn't just speculation—it's something we're already seeing in industries where AI is taking over decision-making.

This raises a difficult but necessary debate: Should AI-driven companies be regulated like public utilities, ensuring that their benefits are shared more broadly? Should ownership models shift toward cooperatives, government-managed AI, or decentralized AI systems to prevent extreme wealth concentration?

There are no easy answers, but ignoring the issue would be a mistake. If Companies of Zero become the norm, we will have to decide whether we want a future of shared prosperity or a world where wealth and control belong to a select few who own the algorithms that run everything.

New Opportunities

Automation won't just eliminate jobs—it will also create new ones. The economy will shift toward industries that **require human creativity, emotional intelligence, and decision-making.**

Some possible new roles:

- **AI Supervisors** – People who monitor and adjust AI behavior

- **AI Ethics Specialists** – Experts who ensure AI follows ethical guidelines
- **Human-AI Collaboration Designers** – Professionals who create ways for people and AI to work together
- **Experience Designers** – Workers who focus on human interaction, storytelling, and creativity in a fully automated world

Some people might choose **entrepreneurship**, using AI to start businesses with minimal costs. Others could focus on **science, entertainment, or research**, areas where human curiosity still drives progress.

Shifts in Global Power

AI-driven companies could reshape entire industries. Nations that develop and control the best AI systems might dominate the global economy. Countries that rely on manual labor or traditional industries could struggle to compete.

A fully automated company doesn't need to outsource work. Manufacturing, logistics, and even financial services could be controlled from anywhere, making location less important. This could disrupt economies that depend on cheap labor or large workforces.

Governments and institutions would need to rethink policies on trade, education, and economic growth to keep up with these changes.

What Happens Next?

The rise of fully autonomous companies will force society to make big decisions. Should there be limits on automation? Should AI-driven businesses pay higher taxes to compensate for job losses? Should governments step in to regulate AI ownership or create publicly managed AI systems to prevent extreme wealth concentration? These aren't just theoretical questions—they're issues we will have to deal with sooner than we think.

If Companies of Zero become common, society will need to redesign work, wealth distribution, and the role of humans in the economy. This isn't just about keeping businesses running—it's about ensuring that the benefits of automation are shared fairly.

One option is to rethink how we measure economic success. If AI-driven businesses can operate without human workers, should economic systems still be based on jobs and wages? Some propose moving toward models where wealth is distributed through public funds, universal basic income, or shared AI ownership. Others argue that governments should heavily regulate AI-driven companies to ensure that they serve the public good rather than just maximizing profits for a few owners.

There is also the question of how much autonomy AI companies should have. If AI agents run everything from financial markets to healthcare to global logistics, should there be human oversight at key decision points? Should we require AI-driven businesses to publish their decision-making processes to ensure accountability?

Beyond economics, there is a deeper cultural shift. What happens to human purpose when work is no longer central to daily life? Will people spend more time on education, creativity, and personal projects, or will automation leave large parts of the population disconnected, dependent, and without a clear role in society?

These are difficult questions with no easy answers. But one thing is clear: doing nothing is not an option. If we let automation shape society without any planning, we could end up with a world where a handful of corporations control nearly all resources, while most people struggle to find meaning and financial stability.

The challenge isn't just to create efficient businesses—it's to ensure that the transition to automation leads to a better society for everyone. This means making proactive choices before AI-driven companies become too powerful to regulate.

In the end, the future of automation isn't just about what AI can do—it's about what kind of world we want to build.

Chapter 15

The Future of Innovation and Entrepreneurship

AI agents won't just change businesses—they will change how we innovate. A world filled with autonomous companies doesn't mean the end of human creativity. It means we get to redefine what it means to be an entrepreneur.

For most of history, starting a business required capital, time, and labor. Founders had to hire teams, manage logistics, and handle daily operations. But in a world where AI agents can run entire companies, anyone with an idea can bring it to life.

A New Kind of Entrepreneurship

Imagine you want to launch a fashion brand, a film studio, or a biotech startup. Instead of hiring employees, you assemble a team of AI agents. One handles product design, another manages marketing, and a third takes care of financial strategy. The company runs 24/7, without the constraints of human schedules or burnout.

This means barriers to entry disappear. You don't need investors to fund an expensive workforce. You don't need years of experience in a field. All you need is a vision. AI agents take care of the execution.

Entrepreneurship could shift from who can afford to build a company to who has the best ideas. This could lead to a surge of innovation, where people from all backgrounds launch projects that would have been impossible in the past.

New businesses wouldn't be limited by geography. An AI-driven startup could source materials, manage supply chains, and serve customers globally from day one. Small businesses that once struggled to compete with industry giants would have AI-powered efficiency on their side, making it possible for them to operate at the same level as multinational corporations.

This could also redefine freelancing and side projects. Right now, launching a business often means taking a financial risk, quitting a stable job, and dedicating years to making it work. But in a world where AI agents handle operations, entrepreneurs could run multiple ventures at once—testing ideas, refining strategies, and pivoting when needed.

It wouldn't just be about building a single company. Individuals could run a portfolio of AI-led businesses, each operating independently while the human founder provides strategic direction. The definition of a "business owner" could shift from someone actively managing a company to someone curating and overseeing multiple AI-driven ventures.

Even collaboration between entrepreneurs could look different. Instead of hiring employees or forming traditional partnerships, founders could connect their AI-driven companies, creating networks of autonomous businesses that share resources, exchange insights, and work together in real time.

This kind of ecosystem would make entrepreneurship more accessible than ever. It wouldn't matter whether someone had the right connections or financial backing—AI agents would level the playing field, giving more people the opportunity to turn their ideas into reality.

The Acceleration of Discovery

One of the biggest impacts of AI-led companies will be in scientific research and technology development. Right now, breakthroughs in fields like medicine, space exploration, and clean energy are held back by bureaucracy, funding limitations, and human error. Even with the best tools, research is often slow, requiring years of testing, peer review, and regulatory approvals before discoveries can be applied in the real world.

But what happens when AI-driven labs can simulate experiments, analyze results, and refine ideas at speeds far beyond human capability? Instead of waiting a decade for new drugs to reach the market, AI could shrink that timeline to weeks or months. Instead of spending years building prototypes for renewable energy solutions, AI could run millions of virtual tests instantly, identifying the best possible designs before a single real-world experiment is conducted.

AI-led research could push humanity toward faster, more efficient solutions to global challenges. Climate change, disease eradication, and space travel aren't limited by our ideas—they're limited by time and resources. AI doesn't have those constraints. A self-sustaining, AI-driven research company could continuously generate and test new theories, refine technology, and propose innovative solutions, operating 24/7 without the delays of traditional human-led institutions.

I see this shift as one of the greatest opportunities of our time. Science has always been about trial and error, but AI removes many of the barriers that make the process slow. It can process massive datasets, detect patterns, and propose hypotheses at speeds we can't match. And the best part? It can work alongside us, helping researchers test ideas, generate insights, and make discoveries that would otherwise take generations.

There's a fear that AI will replace human scientists, but I see it differently. AI won't replace curiosity—it will amplify it. The future isn't about choosing between human ingenuity and artificial intelligence—it's about combining them. AI won't just run companies—it will collaborate with us to solve the world's biggest problems. And that's something to be genuinely excited about.

Work Without Limits

People often assume that if AI replaces human labor, we will all be left without purpose. But I don't think that's the future we're heading toward. Instead of taking something away from us, AI could give us back something we've always craved—time. Time to create, time to explore, time to focus on what makes us human.

For centuries, work has been about survival. People have had to trade their time and energy for money, often doing repetitive or exhausting tasks just to get by. But what happens when those tasks no longer require human effort? What happens when AI agents can run businesses, manage operations, and handle logistics without us needing to be there? Suddenly, we aren't working just to survive—we're working because we want to build something meaningful.

This shift could spark a new era of human creativity and innovation. Imagine a world where people are free to pursue ideas without financial risk, where anyone can start a project without worrying about how they'll pay the bills. AI could handle the day-to-day execution, allowing humans to focus on what really matters—big ideas, creative expression, and pushing the boundaries of knowledge.

Instead of spending hours writing reports, managing spreadsheets, or optimizing supply chains, people could dedicate their time to storytelling, mentoring, problem-solving, and exploration. Scientists could work on understanding the origins of life, artists could push the limits of creative expression, and communities could come together to build new ways of living and working.

For the first time in history, we could move beyond the idea that work is something we have to do and redefine it as something we choose to do. Work could become about personal growth, contribution, and curiosity rather than survival. People could switch careers more freely, experiment with new ideas, and pursue lifelong learning without the pressure of financial instability.

I believe this could be the greatest shift in human history. The world wouldn't just be more efficient—it would be more human. AI isn't here to take away our purpose; it's here to give us the freedom to redefine it.

This could be the beginning of an era where creativity, curiosity, and human potential finally take center stage. And that's a future worth looking forward to.

The Road Ahead

The transition to a world of AI-led businesses won't be smooth. Industries will shift, jobs will change, and traditional economic structures will be challenged. Some people will resist these changes, fearing the uncertainty that comes with automation. But history shows us that every major technological breakthrough—from the industrial revolution to the internet—has transformed society in ways we never imagined. AI will be no different.

There will be disruptions, but there will also be new opportunities. Entirely new industries will emerge, just as they did with the rise of the digital economy. The skills that matter will evolve, shifting from execution to strategy, creativity, and ethical oversight. Instead of fighting automation, we should be asking how we shape it to work for everyone.

This is not a time to fear AI—it's a time to define its role in society. Governments will need to create policies that ensure AI-driven businesses contribute to the well-being of all, not just a select few. Education systems must adapt, teaching people not just how to work with AI, but how to think critically, innovate, and explore new frontiers. We must decide whether AI becomes a tool for progress or a force that deepens inequality.

I believe that AI isn't here to take away what makes us human—it's here to amplify it. Companies of Zero won't just be about automation; they will be about expanding what's possible. If we embrace AI as a partner rather than a replacement, we can build a world where technology empowers people rather than rendering them obsolete.

This is our moment to steer AI in the right direction—to use it not just for efficiency, but for creativity, discovery, and the benefit of all. If we get this right, the future won't be defined by machines taking over. It will be defined by what humans do when freed from limitations.

And that's a future worth building.

Bibliography

The following sources provided valuable insights, frameworks, and examples that shaped the discussions in this book. From AI agent architectures to economic implications, these references offer deeper exploration into the themes of *Companies of Zero*.

AI Agents and Autonomous Systems

Anthropic. *Building Effective AI Agents: Lessons from Real-World Applications.* https://www.anthropic.com

- Galileo AI. *A Field Guide to AI Agents: Understanding Different Types of AI Systems.* https://www.galileo.ai/blog/a-field-guide-to-ai-agents

- Ampcome. *24 Use Cases of AI Agents in Business.* https://www.ampcome.com/post/24-use-cases-of-ai-agents-in-business

- LangChain. *LangGraph and AI Agent Frameworks for Automation.* https://www.langchain.com

Economics and Business Models in AI-Driven Companies

- Brynjolfsson, Erik, and Andrew McAfee. *The Second Machine Age: Work, Progress, and Prosperity in a Time of Brilliant Technologies.* W. W. Norton & Company, 2014.

- Tegmark, Max. *Life 3.0: Being Human in the Age of Artificial Intelligence.* Knopf, 2017.

- Kelly, Kevin. *The Inevitable: Understanding the 12 Technological Forces That Will Shape Our Future.* Viking, 2016.

- Ford, Martin. *Rise of the Robots: Technology and the Threat of a Jobless Future.* Basic Books, 2015.

The Future of Work and AI-Driven Innovation

- Ravikant, Naval. *The Almanack of Naval Ravikant: A Guide to Wealth and Happiness.* Magrathea Publishing, 2020.

- Levels, Pieter. *MAKE: The Indie Maker Handbook.* Self-published, 2021.

- Altman, Sam. *AI and the Future of Startups.* https://blog.samaltman.com

- Paul Graham. *Essays on Startups and Entrepreneurship.* https://paulgraham.com

Ethical Considerations and AI Governance

- Russell, Stuart. *Human Compatible: Artificial Intelligence and the Problem of Control.* Viking, 2019.

- Bostrom, Nick. *Superintelligence: Paths, Dangers, Strategies.* Oxford University Press, 2014.

- Floridi, Luciano. *The Ethics of Artificial Intelligence: Principles and Policy Recommendations.* Oxford Internet Institute, 2020.

- Various Authors. *OECD Principles on AI: Policy Considerations for AI Regulation and Ethics.* OECD, 2019.

Real-World Applications of AI in Business

- Amazon Web Services. *AI in Enterprise: Bedrock AI and Autonomous Business Models.* https://aws.amazon.com/bedrock

- OpenAI. *Exploring the Future of AI-Powered Businesses.* https://www.openai.com

- HubSpot. *The Role of AI in Sales and Marketing Automation.* https://blog.hubspot.com

- Google DeepMind. *AI Research and the Future of Work.* https://deepmind.com

This bibliography represents a mix of academic research, industry insights, and thought leadership in artificial intelligence, business automation, and economic shifts driven by AI. These works helped shape the vision presented in *Companies of Zero*, offering a glimpse into a future where AI-powered businesses redefine what it means to work, create, and innovate.

ABOUT THE AUTHOR

Daniel Locke is an entrepreneur and technologist with a deep passion for AI-driven businesses and automation. With a background in computer science and over 20 years in the financial industry, Daniel witnessed firsthand how technology reshapes industries. After leaving the world of corporate finance, he set out to explore how AI could run companies independently, managing operations, optimizing decision-making, and redefining entrepreneurship.

Fascinated by the idea of autonomous companies, Daniel studies how AI agents can replace traditional business structures. Inspired by thought leaders like Sam Altman, Paul Graham, Naval Ravikant, and Pieter Levels, he has made it his mission to share insights on how AI is not just a tool—but a new way of thinking about business itself.

In Companies of Zero, Daniel takes readers into the world of AI-led organizations, showing how businesses can scale without human employees and what this means for the future of work, innovation, and society. He blends technical expertise with real-world experience, offering an optimistic but realistic view of how AI can empower entrepreneurs, researchers, and creatives.

A lifelong fan of science fiction, automation, and big ideas, Daniel believes that AI isn't here to replace human ingenuity—it's here to amplify it.

You can connect with Daniel on Twitter: @Daniel_ZZ80 or reach out via email at daniellockeyyy@gmail.com for questions, insights, or collaborations.